THE POTENTIAL OF

FORM   HOW TO TRANSFORM EXISTING BUILDINGS
        IN POST-FUNCTIONAL EUROPE

ELENA GUIDETTI

jovis

THE POTENTIAL OF

FORM   HOW TO TRANSFORM EXISTING BUILDINGS
                IN POST-FUNCTIONAL EUROPE

                ELENA GUIDETTI

jovis

Introduction	A feeling for the potential	7
	Acknowledgments	14

AAA POTENTIAL(S): ANCESTRY, ARCHITECTURE, AND ADAPTATIONS — 19

Potential as a cross-disciplinary concept:
unfolding a concept — 20

Precedents for the potential in architecture:
looking for potentials — 29

A transformative potential of form:
toward a new methodology — 42

Cross-lenses in post-functional frameworks:
setting the rules — 54

AR POST-FUNCTIONAL FORMS: ADAPTIVE REUSE PROJECTS THROUGH STAGES OF COMPLETENESS — 63

Footprints — 66
Duperré Playground — 68
Can Tacò — 72
Can Sau — 76
Basilica di Siponto — 80

Structures — 84
Kraanspoor — 86
King's Cross Gasholders — 90
Vitali Sheds — 94
Panorâmico de Monsanto — 98

Shells — 102
Alvéoles — 104
Cité de la Mode et du Design — 108
Szimpla Kert — 112
PC Caritas — 116

Boxes — 120
Bourse du Commerce — 122
Bookshop Dominicanen — 126
Elbphilharmonie — 130
Hôtel-Dieu — 134

COMPARATIVE TABLES: TIME OPPORTUNITIES, SPATIAL PATTERNS, AND ENERGY DYNAMICS OF FORM — 141

Conclusions	Toward sustainable forms of transformations	153
	Glossary relating to potential	174
References		178
Afterword	by Matteo Robiglio	183
Imprint		184

INTRODUCTION:
A FEELING FOR THE POTENTIAL

Adaptation is the timeless story of transforming objects, buildings, cities, and landscapes, recognizing their potential not merely to be preserved as they are or were, but to be transformed and live another life. This narrative spans a broad spectrum of reuse—from material and component repurposing to basic repair, refurbishment, remodeling, repositioning, conversion, and restoration—, all within the ongoing debate on preservation and transformation, which is now central to sustainability concerns.

This book traces the concept of potential through a concise interdisciplinary overview and explores the transformative potential embedded in the architectural form of buildings that have undergone adaptive reuse. It examines a variety of approaches to building reuse, focusing on the states of (in)completeness of the "as found"[1] form and the evolution of morphological features. By analyzing the "potential" as the relationship between these elements, the book offers an interdisciplinary lens for interpreting the continuous evolution of our built environment.

Background talks

When it comes to urban legacies, the conversation extends beyond the academic realm of preservation, cultural heritage, and decision-making studies related to existing buildings. In the current Western context, nations, institutions, and policymakers also have to address the complexities of managing the built environment to meet present-day needs, particularly in light of climate change. (United Nations 2015) In the past ten years, particularly in the European context, the phenomenon of reusing existing buildings has increased, and since 2010, the EU renovation market has overtaken the domain of new buildings. (Saheb 2016, 14) In March 2024, the Energy Performance of Buildings Directive (EPBD) by the European Parliament marked an important turn in the EU Renovation Wave, setting a number of policies designed to boost the energy efficiency of buildings, including the increase of retrofitting to meet decarbonization goals. (EU/2024/1275) Despite common agreement regarding the reuse of existing buildings as a driver of sustainability in the construction industry, this industry still has the unfortunate role of being the largest consumer of resources and raw materials.[2] The choice of preserving a structure that has required the use of resources is even more relevant considering the framework of environmental sustainability. In view of the scarcity of natural resources and the development of greenfield areas, adapting instead of demolishing and rebuilding plays a crucial role in fostering the sustainable conservation of the resources embedded in the urban fabric and brownfield sites. On the wave of "New ideas must use old buildings" (Jacobs 1961, 188), the reuse of existing buildings is today a crucial challenge worldwide: Old seems to be the new New.[3]

Large-scale events increasingly reflect a growing awareness of the need to reuse existing venues to minimize their carbon footprint. For example, the Olympic Games have shifted their focus from constructing new venues to reusing existing ones. Paris 2024 had committed to using 95% of existing or temporary infrastructures for the Olympic and Paralympic Games, integrating monuments and the landscape itself as part of the venues. Los Angeles 2028 aims to push this concept even further, with the IOC declaring that 100% of the venues will be pre-existing, embodying an even more radical approach to reuse.[4]

In the European Agenda, the objective "Sustainable Cities and Communities" is the 11th of the 17 Sustainable Development Goals (SDGs) established by the United Nations General Assembly in 2015. Among the targets and indicators of the SDGs, Target 11.4 specifically aims to "protect the world's cultural and natural heritage." This target highlights the integral relationship between sustainability and the sustainable development of cities.[5] In the European context, the renovation of public and private buildings is a critical action that has been identified in the European Green Deal as a crucial effort to improve the sector's energy efficiency and meet requirements. In fact, within the European context, adaptive reuse is currently one of the central subjects of several projects on the EU Agenda.[6] Indeed, the increasing attention being paid to adaptive reuse in both academia and the construction industry demonstrates this topic's growing relevance in architectural theory and practice.

Governments have put effort into drawing guidelines for the renovation of building stock that is not meeting contemporary needs.[7] Adaptive capacity is increasingly a matter of public interest, yet different policy systems across Europe impact the feasibility of adaptive reuse. These policy systems also signal varying attitudes toward adaptive reuse itself, rooted in the cultural, social, and economic aspects of each country, reflecting a lack of consensus on how best to approach existing buildings.[8] In the present era, more than ever, the integration of sustainability concerns into the preservationist debate is a crucial topic in contemporary architectural discourse.[9] In the Western context, the preservation argument has recently expanded to the reuse of existing buildings, regardless of their official heritage label as a function of embracing the sustainability agenda. (Elefante 2012)

Deciding what should be preserved and how to preserve it has been an evolving process, rooted in a long and extensive historical tradition.[10] Besides, the idea of preserving "obsolete forms" even if not suitable for current needs is a quite recent concern, even in European culture. (Stubbs 2009) Thus, even without recognizing any heritage value in a current urban legacy, the complete demolition of any historical building to make way for new architecture still seems unthinkable. While it is a matter of fact that "preservation is overtaking us," (Koolhaas et al. 2014) the call for "Never demolish, never remove or replace, always add, transform, and reuse!…"[11] supports the recognition of adaptive reuse as the "New Normal" in architectural interventions. (Schittich 2003, 9) Adding, aggregating, combining, expanding, overlaying, and assembling to improve what is already there is very effective in extending the lifespan of existing structures; such urban architectural and landscape infrastructures already exist, and we must take advantage of them. (Lacaton and Vassal 2011)

Blurring the boundaries

The boundaries of the modern preservation debate are increasingly blurred, positioning adaptive reuse as a key process in promoting the sustainable conservation of resources embedded in the urban fabric. In the academic framework, a bibliometric analysis (conducted from 2010 to 2020) has demonstrated a growing interest in combining heritage, adaptive reuse, and sustainable development into a holistic approach to foster both conservation and development. (Li et al. 2021) The adaptive reuse of heritage buildings is becoming increasingly popular; as commentators have noted, this popularity can in part be attributed to the economic, cultural, and social benefits they provide to urban communities. In considering adaptive reuse, urban developers and planners seek to reach an equilibrium in the battle between time and space. Both academically and practically, the adaptive reuse of heritage buildings requires compatible, appropriate, and scientific means for assessing built heritage assets; however, currently, research in this area is still relatively meagre. To address this gap, this paper investigates research frameworks, methodologies, and assessment methods that concern the adaptive reuse of architectural heritage. In this paper, we examine the current literature on the paradigms for applying mixed methodologies: the multi-criteria decision model (MCDM). However, little effort has been made as to how preservation studies can be integrated into the sustainability discourse. Despite the overall positive impact of adaptive reuse, (Langston 2008) integral conservation is neither feasible in cultural, social, environmental, and economic terms nor conducive to fostering the evolution of our cities to achieve resilience and progress. (Seekamp and Jo 2020; Holtorf 2018; Ashworth 1997)

Adaptive reuse, as both a discipline and a field of theory and practice, is increasingly gaining prominence in playing across disciplinary boundaries. Since the 1970s, the debate on adaptive reuse has primarily focused on mapping architectural phenomena and providing tools and strategies for practitioners and designers. However, recent works are shifting toward a more conceptual investigation of adaptive reuse, potentially inviting contributions from disciplines beyond architecture and design. (Stone 2023) As Sally Stone pointed out, a precise definition of adaptive reuse is currently non-existent and perhaps unnecessary. Adaptive reuse can be viewed as a branch of architecture that focuses on transforming existing buildings to meet new needs. Within this field, it is possible to include the reuse and recycling of certain building components,[12] along with the conscious acceptance of loss and decay as part of any adaptation strategy.[13]

Here, adaptive reuse is meant as any process of reusing an obsolete and derelict building by changing its function to maximize the reuse and retention of existing materials and structures according to the design intervention to meet current users' needs.[14] Therefore, this definition includes buildings not labeled as heritage and, as such, not acknowledged as objects of preservation in the narrow sense.[15] Consequently, this work focuses on built legacy, which also accounts for heritage discourse, and enlarges the idea of adaptive reuse itself by considering the generative power of non-interventional and even destructive practices.[16] Such practices are adaptive reuse interventions or part of their process.[17] Moreover, the call for incorporating embodied carbon studies and embodied energy analysis can be highly beneficial for exploring a wide range of possibilities in adaptive reuse interventions. This approach supports the sustainable use of resources and promotes a holistic framework for adaptive reuse itself. (Wong 2023, 228–38; Cairns and Jacobs 2014, 220–32)

Adaptive reuse, when broadly considered, can transform built legacies by addressing the dichotomies of preservation versus demolition and heritage versus transformation. This approach aligns with decarbonization goals by incorporating environmental engineering studies focused on embodied energy and embodied carbon throughout the adaptation process. (Guidetti and Ferrara 2023) Looking within the disciplinary boundaries of adaptive reuse, it is evident that the quest to convert structures to meet current needs has traditionally been linked to typological forms, functional categories, and technical specifications.[18] (Plevoets and Van Cleempoel 2013) It is clear that there are overlaps between these categories, which serve to deepen the understanding and complexity of real-world phenomena.

In architecture, the classification of buildings into typologies to analyze existing architecture and foster eventual interventions first emerged in the classical treatises spanning from Vitruvius to Durand. (Krinsky 1989; Durand and Legrand 1801; Durand 1809) In adaptive reuse theory, a well-established field analyzes existing buildings on the basis of functional classification (i.e., residential, industrial, commercial, or religious). Thus, focusing on the evolution of form to meet users' needs appears to be a more promising perspective when analyzing architectural objects undergoing adaptations, especially when the original function is no longer active. Quoting Louis Kahn's remarks (1965), dismissed buildings can be considered post-functional "vessels of memory free from function constraints" and valuable in terms of their inherent qualities. (Latour 1991, 197–219) In general, we could regard the original function of a building as relatively irrelevant when it comes to alterations, focusing instead on how these spaces can be newly inhabited while its form incorporates changes over time. (Brooker 2021, 31–32; Scott 2008; Brand 1995) Nevertheless, little attention has been paid to testing a morphological approach in adaptive reuse, (Fisher-Gewirtzman 2016) especially concerning the integration between a form-form relationship[19] and a more practical approach within a practical approach to morphological studies. (Ching 1979; Clark and Pause 1985)

Shall we then blur the lines? Sustainability and preservation, architecture and heritage studies, adaptive reuse and environmental energy studies, as well as architectural design and morphological analysis, are all seamlessly intertwined in a transformative approach.

Outlining the vision

What if we approached the transformation of existing buildings not through the lens of functional typologies or historical values but by focusing on their "potentials"? This book proposes to explore a morphological approach through time by engaging the concept of potential. Such a shift of perspective in evaluating the existing built environment is based on what existing buildings can physically become in terms of form, despite what they originally were in functional terms. It is a partial angle on the process of adaptive reuse but still an attempt to embrace a shift of perspective based on mutual relationships. Thus, the concept of potential(s), which has been highlighted as crucial in adaptive reuse discourse, emerges as essential. This shift could be beneficial in outlining a trend embedded in existing buildings, and it might facilitate adaptive reuse as an inclusive practice capable of fostering a transformative approach within the preservation field meant as "conservation," seeking a proper use of existing buildings, instead of protecting them from use.[20]

This book aims to introduce and define some "transformative potentials" of existing buildings through a post-functional perspective in the European context. Specifically, this work defines existing buildings—both heritage-listed and not—in terms of "potential." The research challenges disciplinary boundaries but leads to considering one angle within the complexity of the adaptive reuse processes by focusing only on the physical aspects of buildings. In doing so, the impact of functional purpose, symbolic and heritage values are not considered. The building's form is therefore investigated, regardless of legal, normative, heritage, symbolic value, and functional concerns.

The choice to place this research in "post-functional Europe" refers both to the geographic-cultural context of this analysis and to the object of analysis. Specifically, "post-functional" means uncharacterized by its original functional purpose. In other words, the scope of this book is within the European context of contemporary intervention on buildings that are not (anymore) characterized by a stable functional purpose. This "post-functional" condition is undeniable in the case of dismissed buildings that are eventually adapted to accommodate new uses.[21]

Evaluating a built structure in terms of potential means shifting the approach from asking "what does it mean" to "what does it do" (Reiser and Umemoto 2006, 23) and "how." Here, the proposal is to deconstruct the classical typological classification and put a morphological framework in its place, assuming the questionable role of the new building over the sheer amount of built stock in the present. As Goethe's archetypal plant is presented in terms of potential, where elements comprise a complex system, it might be defined by its capabilities to evolve instead of using deductive reasoning to categorize it a priori. (von Goethe 1790)

To embrace an inductive approach, this book attempts to first explore the theoretical concept of potential; although it has been widely applied within the narrative surrounding adaptive reuse studies, it still has a nebulous meaning. Many authors refer to the concept of "potential" in general terms, where the "untapped potential" in existing buildings is an unstated value waiting to be released. (Douglas 2006) However, the act of rescuing such an "untapped potential" of dismissed buildings emerges as an adaptation goal. By referring to post-preservation and counter-preservation, as well as non-intervention practices, the concept of potential is closely connected with the meaning of unavoidable change by non-architects, nature, and time. (Hughes and Sadler 2000; Sandler 2016; DeSilvey 2017)

The hypothesis presented in this book explores the transformative potential of architectural form, considering it as a state of (temporary) equilibrium between spatial structure and materials. (Borie, Micheloni, and Pinon 1978; Reiser and Umemoto 2006; Rossi 1981; Ching 1979) This "equilibrium" changes and evolves through time under decay processes and through architectural interventions. Time is deemed a proper physical dimension of architecture that actualizes itself through the decay of the material that makes up the building. (Abramson 2016; Cairns and Jacobs 2014) Finally, through the assumption of an ideal-type-based model, schematizations of reality simplify such a complex system, which is otherwise not transmissible in design applications. (Weber et al. 1949, 194; Moles 1951) This novel reading of the process of adaptive reuse of existing buildings will be explored through the lens of (de)constructive actions, which have an impact in terms of the use of resources and sustainability.

Interdisciplinary lenses

The vision outlined initiates a preliminary conversation, asking: What if we embraced an interdisciplinary approach, testing its value to explore new possibilities and uncover eventual pathways? This work relies on a multiple case study analysis, which combines three methods from diverse fields of studies (morphology, adaptive reuse, environmental engineering) and intensive fieldwork documented through a digital atlas of examples.[22]

In the field of architecture, a case study methodology is a well-established approach in the adaptive reuse field. (Plevoets and Van Cleempoel 2019; Barasch 2019; Robiglio 2017; Wong 2016; Jäger 2010; Brooker and Stone 2004) Starting with Durand's plates, case studies have become a scientific methodology within academia.[23] This study reviews sixteen well-known adapted buildings that emerged in the European context within the last fifteen years. The cases presented here are not organized according to the functional classification of existing buildings, historical periods, or heritage labels. Instead, the selection process focused on original buildings from various epochs and functional types. The criteria for selection included the degree of decay of the existing structure at the time of adaptive reuse design, as well as the diversity of dimensional and structural configurations. Such a morpho-structural variety follows the logic of the Weberian *Idealtypus*, (Weber et al. 1949) which represents an unreal conceptual framework that serves as a template or a scheme of reality disclosing its significant elements. Such an ex-post draft classification of existing buildings as morpho-structural types is a preliminary test that could lead to the expansion of future findings to the whole category.

Considering morphological and structural conditions crucial in delivering adaptation projects, (Douglas 2006) the book encompasses various intervention theory approaches (White 1999; Brooker and Stone 2004; Jäger 2010; Robert 1989; Wong 2016) and includes minimal intervention and ruination (Plevoets and Van Cleempoel 2019) as a design possibility. Thus, the cases include adaptation projects with interventions ranging from radical to minimal that started from a diverse stage of decay of the original building. These 16 cases are located on the route of an intensive 40-day fieldwork session around Europe, conducted during the summer of 2021. This research journey was motivated not only by the desire to explore the case studies but also by the intention to collect a large number of examples of building adaptation (more than 40) and several unexpected cases (more than 20) to start building an open atlas with geo-references and tags.[24]

The lens applied to these projects integrates multiple investigation methodologies, combining architectural studies on building morphology with adaptive reuse research and exploring the application of embodied energy in existing buildings. This interdisciplinary approach inherently simplifies each individual discipline, recognizing that such integration may introduce limitations that could impact the results when viewed from a strictly monodisciplinary perspective. The methods applied integrate 1) decay stage evaluation, 2) morphological analysis, and 3) retroactive embodied energy assessment.

The first method of decay evaluation involves "shearing layers." (Brand 1995; Duffy 1992; Kuipers and de Jonge 2017) Here, the method is intended to assess the building integrity in time, starting from how many layers are in place before and after the adaptive reuse intervention. Such a method constructs and investigates four families of cases. This analysis assumes that decay influences the presence of shearing layers and their relative completeness and that not all these layers may be required to define a "building."

The second method, morphological analysis, consists of the critical redrawing of original buildings and highlights the dimensional features (Ching 1979; Clark and Pause 1985) and configurational aspects. (Kurrent 1978; Marshall 2005; Guidetti and Massarente 2021) The building, in its urban context, is analyzed through schemes, which propose a simplification of reality that makes the physical evolution and the "deformation" that takes place through a design process evident. (Borie et al. 1978). The redrawing follows a similar approach to the yellow-red color code, to underline the architectural projects built on preexisting architecture.[25] (Boesch et al. 2019)

The third method, retroactive embodied energy analysis, retraces the preserved, added, removed, or replaced materials during the adaptive reuse process. (Jackson 2005; Benjamin 2017; Guidetti and Ferrara 2023) The embodied energy assessment utilizes a simplified version of the input-output analysis model, focusing exclusively on the primary structural materials. (Advisory Council on Historical Preservation 1979)

Structure of the book

This book marks the first step in proposing the concept of potential within an adaptive reuse framework, testing this concept through several case studies, and drawing conclusions to be expanded upon based on identified weaknesses and limitations. The volume is organized into three main chapters, final remarks, and an appendix.

Chapter One—"AAA Potential(s)"—delves into the concept of potential, offering a critical literature review that traces its evolution across multiple disciplines. It identifies key features of potential as shared behaviors among diverse contexts, culminating in the field of adaptive reuse. The transformative potential examined here is based on the physical characteristics of existing buildings that have undergone adaptive reuse. It is presented as a measure of building form evolution, both qualitative and quantitative, in terms of morphology and materials, analyzed from diachronic and trans-scalar perspectives.

Chapter Two—"AR Post-functional Forms"—analyzes 16 case studies, introduced by a brief toolbox explaining the integrated methodology and post-functional framework applied. The cases are organized into four subchapters—"Footprints," "Structures," "Shells," and "Boxes"—following the layers' completeness of each building "as found" before adaptive reuse intervention. Each building's adaptation is examined using a detailed analysis form.

Chapter Three—with the "Comparative Tables"—discusses the findings through a cross-comparison of the cases, examining de(constructive) actions in both quantitative and qualitative terms. This leads to the development of trajectories of form evolution over time, highlighting adaptive reuse interventions that transform the space and substance of existing buildings.

The book concludes with a broad classification of transformative potentials and their applications in adaptive reuse practice. These potentials are described in terms of the equilibrium between the completeness of the existing building, design actions, and sustainability. The appendix includes a glossary of key terms and a list of references to support the reader. This book invites readers to explore how spatial possibilities evolve through changes in their morphological and material conditions.

ACKNOWLEDGMENTS

This book would not have been possible without the invaluable support I received from the Future *Urban Legacy* Lab (F*UL*L), the interdepartmental research center at Politecnico di Torino, where I began my PhD in November 2018 and continue collaborating as a post-doctoral researcher. The manuscript you are holding is a distilled version of the thesis developed at this center, reflecting the limitations inherent in such an ex-post reduction. I am profoundly grateful to Politecnico di Torino and the PhD program "Architecture. History and Project" (DASP) for providing the foundation and support necessary to develop and refine this research.

I owe special thanks to Matteo Robiglio, who supervised my PhD research and graciously agreed to write the afterword to this book. Our collaboration began over a cup of excellent coffee in Turin, where Matteo encouraged me to explore the concept of potential in adaptive reuse. Since then, he has provided me with unfailing support while also granting me the invaluable freedom to chart my own course.

My heartfelt gratitude goes to Bie Plevoets from Hasselt University for her insightful review of the original thesis and her invaluable feedback during my visit to Hasselt in 2022. I also extend my deepest thanks to Alessandro Massarente, who has supported my academic path since I was a student at the University of Ferrara. Since then, our collaboration has been a continuous source of inspiration in research and teaching.

I am deeply thankful to Elena Vigliocco for her insightful feedback on the draft of this work and her constant willingness to engage in thoughtful discussions throughout my research journey. Her open approach has played a key role in shaping this project and, I hope, many more to come. I also wish to express my sincere gratitude to Caitlin DeSilvey, Sara Marini, Alexandre Monnin, and Emanuele Morezzi for their thoughtful critiques during the revision and defense of my PhD thesis. Their perspectives have broadened my understanding of the topic and significantly enhanced the coherence and depth of this book. I extend my gratitude to Nina Rapport for her inspiring insights, which began during her teaching visit to Turin in 2019 and continue to this day. I am also grateful to Cornelius Holtorf and Daniela Sandler for their participation in seminars in Turin in 2022, which greatly influenced my research perspective on preservation theory.

A special thank you is due to all the researchers and friends at the F*UL*L research center and the Department of Architecture and Design at Politecnico di Torino for their continuous feedback and for fostering an interdisciplinary exchange that is all too rare in our field.

This book would also not have been possible without the generosity of the architects who provided access to archives, original drawings, and, most importantly, their time. Their support, encountered throughout my fieldwork across Europe, was both kind and invaluable. I am deeply thankful for their collaboration on the projects cited here.

I must also thank Studio Faire in the persons of Colin and Julia, along with my co-residents Ben, Dina, and Jane for the enriching artist and writer residency experience in Neràc in the summer of 2024, which gave a significant boost to my writing.

Lastly, I extend my gratitude to all my families. My beloved natural first family, who have always supported me (no matter what), and allowed me to follow my path, unwaveringly fostering my independence; my irreplaceable "family by choice," from long before architecture was on my radar, including Ambra, Alice, Chiara, Elena, Francesca, Ginevra, Guendalina, Giovanni, Martina, Sara, along with Camilla, Caterina, Filippo, Luca, Lucia, Massimiliano, Roberta, and Silvia; and my beautiful extended "family by chance," built during the last decade of studies and research in architecture around the world: Adriano, Agostino, Alberto, Alessia, Alessandro, Andrea, Ayca, Caterina, Chiara, Daniele, Diego,

Elena, Emanuele, Enrico, Federico, Federico, Giulia, Giulia, Ilaria, Laura, Leonie, Lisa, Lucia, Lorenzo, Matteo, Maria, Martina, Massimo, Miquel, Riccardo, Roberta, Sahar, Sigfried, Stella, Valerio, and Valeria for (un)consciously reviewing parts of this book and for often discussing ideas over a glass of wine. Among them, a special mention to Adriano, Federico, Ilaria, Laura, and Matteo for being not just great friends but also actual readers of the very first draft of this work.

Finally, a heartfelt thanks to Franziska, the patient editor of this work at jovis, and an extended apology for any language shortcomings for which I count on the indulgence of native speakers.

Endnotes

1   The concept of "as found" recalls the design methodology of Alison and Peter Smithson, as outlined in their 1990 work. (Smithson and Smithson 1990, 201) This approach is characterized by an "attitude that starts from observation and analysis of the existing," as highlighted in the recent adaptive reuse exhibition titled "As Found: Experiment in Preservation." (De Caigny et al. 2023, 10)

2   Despite the diverse approaches to reuse, Foster highlights the widely recognized potential for social, economic, and environmental benefits. He emphasizes the alignment between the principles of the circular economy and building reuse, focusing on reducing resource extraction and waste while promoting human well-being. Foster demonstrates that extending the lifespan of buildings offers multiple advantages that positively impact the economic and social development of cities. However, decision-makers often lack understanding of the trade-offs between these advantages and the tools available to support informed decision-making.

3   Quoting and reinforcing the idea that adapting existing structures is the "New Normal" underscores how conservation and adaptation are now seen as complementary, not contradictory. (Schittich 2003, 9) This concept also applies to the adaptive reuse of industrial buildings. (Robiglio 2017, 170)

4   Brence Culp, LA2028's Chief Impact Officer states that "the most sustainable venue is the one you don't have to build." See the interview from the IOC (International Olympic Committee) on 04/10/2018. Available at https://olympics.com/ioc/news/la2028-q-a-radical-reuse-in-action. Accessed on 05/08/2024.

5   RenovationWave EU. Available at https://energy.ec.europa.eu/topics/energy-efficiency/energy-efficient-buildings/renovation-wave_en. Accessed on 25/02/2022.

6   See the Leeuwarden Declaration, which is specifically focused on adaptive reuse. Adaptive reuse of built heritage entails preserving and enhancing the values of our built heritage for future generations. See Horizon 2020, Getting Cultural Heritage Work, 2020. Available at https://ec.europa.eu/programmes/horizon2020/en/news/getting-cultural-heritage-work-europe. Accessed on 06/06/2021; OpenHeritage – Organizing, Promoting and Enabling Heritage Re-use through Inclusion, Technology, Access, Governance and Empowerment. Available at https://ec.europa.eu/futurium/en/system/files/ged/d_1.2_mapping_of_current_heritage_reuse_policies_and_regulations_in_europe.pdf. Accessed on 03/08/2024.

7   Mapping of Current Heritage Re-Use Policies and Regulations in Europe: Complex Policy Overview of Adaptive Heritage Re-Use, Open Heritage, December 2019. Available at https://openheritage.eu/resources/. Accessed March 2021.

8   As data shows, for instance, conversation projects in France can also be reuse projects, while in Flanders, there is a growing policy push for adaptive reuse. In England, adaptive reuse is not mentioned in policy as a term, but as a practice it is normalized; in Germany, adaptive reuse is a common practice, and the national policy program on Urban Heritage Protection has been crucial, similar to the Netherlands, where adaptive reuse is highly supported by the government. On the contrary, in Hungary, the concept of adaptive reuse does not exist in legislative or policy documents. Poland has no specific regulations or other legal basis addressing adaptive heritage reuse. In Spain, there seems to be a general

	positive policy framework that has started to stimulate adaptive reuse to become a common practice, while in Italy, adaptive reuse is connected to aims of solving vacancy and conservation is often seen as a barrier for interventions.
9	In her inaugural Jaqueline Tyrwhitt Urban Design Lecture on March 29, 2022 at Harvard University's Graduate School of Design, Anne Lacaton stated, "Never demolish. Always transform, with and for the inhabitants." The 2021 Pritzker Prize winner emphasized the importance of reusing existing buildings whenever possible. The award, which is the highest honor in architecture, underscores a significant shift in the field towards valuing adaptation as a central element of contemporary practice. The Pritzker Prize jury highlighted that Lacaton & Vassal's work was recognized for starting "every project with a process of discovery that includes intensely observing and finding value in what already exists" and for offering "renewed potential to what already existed." Anne Lacaton also opened the exhibition "As found," focused on the new relationship between contemporary design and heritage. International architecture exhibitions started to consider adaptation as a matter of relevance, including the discourse. Back to the 1997, the exhibition "Architectures Transformées – Renovation and Conversion in Paris" at the Arsenale Pavilion in Venice showed how buildings designed in the past have been adapted either by slight modifications or major interventions. The German contribution to the 13th Venice Architecture Biennale, titled "Reduce/Reuse/Recycle. Architecture as a Resource" showcases sixteen strategies that highlight the significant creative and architectural potential of a positive approach to existing structures. (Petzet and Heilmeyer 2012) Besides, the "Emotional Heritage" exhibition at the Arsenale, curated by Flores y Prat for the Biennale Architettura 2023, explores the centrality of the interventions on existing buildings and engages with the concepts of time, overwriting, fixing, and memory. (Lokko 2023, 152–253)
10	In 1964, the Venice Charter focused on "monuments" as the only architectural objects appropriate to preserve. Nevertheless, the fifth article recognizes the importance of using heritage buildings for some socially useful purposes, even if it would require a change of function for the historical structure. Post-war conservationists started considering the whole historical urban fabric, including vernacular architecture and industrial buildings, as subject to preservation issues due to the massive destruction. (Choay 1992) The role of adaptive reuse in conservation practice was introduced in the 1970s as a means of enlarging the traditional approach to heritage buildings and the object of conservation itself. The built environment could thus be read as a palimpsest, composed of diverse layers from different epochs. (Machado 1976) Thus, this shift from monument to palimpsest might potentially include all the built environment under the preservation domain. (Vecco 2010) Perhaps, heritage borders are now more blurred than ever, and even what is not recognized as heritage can be considered a preservationist concern.
11	Lecaton & Vassal when receiving the 2021 Pritzker Architecture Prize
12	For instance, Philippe Robert proposes "Recycling materials of vestiges" as an adaptive reuse intervention in his book. (Robert 1989)
13	A well-established body of literature evaluates the impact of demolition and building material reuse. (Foster 2020; Thornton 2011; Bullen and Love 2010; Crowther 1999) According to Chusid (1993, 17–20), buildings that are obsolete or rapidly approaching disuse and potential demolition might be a "mine" of raw materials, quantified as "urban ore."
14	This definition is adapted from (Shahi et al. 2020) to encompass a broad range of interventions, emphasizing the evaluation of adaptive reuse as a "process" (Stone 2023) and making clear its connection to sustainability needs. (Wong 2023, 228–38) To get an overview of the state of the art in adaptive reuse studies, see: Lanz and Pendlebury 2022; Stone 2023.
15	The concept of adaptive reuse shares some features with other well-known concepts in preservation (i.e., refurbishment rehabilitation, remodeling, and retrofitting), thus highlighting both the lack of a specialized and agreed-upon terminology within the field and the blurred borders between terms. (Stone 2023; Wong 2023; Shahi et al. 2020; Plevoets and Van Cleempoel 2019; Wong 2016; Douglas 2006)
16	The research group "Heritage Futures," which considers this term "helpful in bringing heritage, which is generally understood to be something which is both endangered and positively valued, into comparative perspective with other more abject forms of remnants, traces, redundant objects and practices, and/or material and discursive residues." See Heritage Futures, Lexicon, available at https://heritage-futures.org/lexicon/#!legacies. Accessed on 08/07/2024. The "Future Urban Legacy Lab" research center considers the term "legacy" as "a situation that exists now because of events, actions, etc., that took place in the past" in particular applied to the urban environment. Available at https://full.polito.it/wp-content/uploads/2021/12/REPORT_2017_2021.pdf. Accessed on 06/01/2024.
17	For instance, the process of "stripping back" is an integral part of any alteration to existing buildings. (Scott 2008, 107–15)
18	These traditional approaches are contingent upon which function is considered suitable according to the typology of the existing building (Machado 1976; Cunnington 1988; Douglas 2006), with a particular emphasis on specific functional types, such as the first adaptive reuses of industrial

buildings. (Robiglio 2017; Stratton 1997; Robert 1989; Cunnington 1988) This so-called "typological approach" (Plevoets and Van Cleempoel 2019, 16) organizes the built environment based on existing functional typologies instead of analyzing the relationship between the morphological adaptation process, the latter of which is free from functional constraints. In contrast, an architectural approach focuses mainly on form-form relationships. (Brooker and Stone 2019; Wong 2016; Bollack 2013; Brooker and Stone 2004; Cramer and Breitling 2007; Jäger 2010; White 1999; Robert 1989)

19 Ibid., 18
20 See "Preservation" in Glossary
21 See "Post-functional" in Glossary
22 See the ongoing project "Atlas of Potential" started by the author in July 2021. Available at https://www.atlasofpotential.com/.
23 Jean-Nicolas-Louis Durand viewed classification into typologies as a tool for critical replication. (Durand 1809) However, since the nineteenth century, architectural research has been recognized as a scientific product because of the application of a "scientific method." (Caballero Lobera 2017) This rationalist-based architecture often employs inductive reasoning based on the observation of a particular phenomenon.
24 Ibid., 23
25 In this case, the BYR code (Black for preserved, Yellow for demolished, Red for added) omits representations of demolitions to enhance the readability of the process.

AAA POTENTIAL(S):

ANCESTRY, ARCHITECTURE, ADAPTATIONS

POTENTIAL AS A CROSS-DISCIPLINARY CONCEPT: UNFOLDING A CONCEPT

> Potential (Adj): Possible as opposed to actual, existing "in posse" or a latent or undeveloped state, capable of coming into being or action, latent. In physics, potential function, potential energy, potential temperature.
> Potential (N): That which is possible, as opposed to what is actual; a possibility. Also, resources that can be used or developed; freq. preceded by a defining word. In Grammar, short form for "potential mood." In Physics, "potential barrier," "potential flow," "potential gradient," "potential scattering," and "potential wall." (Onions 1966, 700–701)

Understanding potential requires an in-depth analysis of its meaning, historical context, and application across different fields. What does potential mean, where does it belong, and how has its meaning evolved over time? This section explores these questions and identifies the main fields of study that utilize this concept.

A survey on the use of the term "potential" across history

The term "potential" is versatile, serving as both an adjective and a noun. It can enhance another term or stand independently. A review of major etymological dictionaries reveals the fascinating evolution of this word:

> The adjective dates back to the late 14c., "possible" (as opposed to *actual*), "capable of being or becoming," from Old French *potenciel* and directly from Medieval Latin *potentialis* "potential," from Latin *potentia* "power, might, force;" figuratively "political power, authority, influence," from *potens* "powerful," from *potis* "powerful, able, capable; possible;" of persons, "better, preferable; chief, principal; strongest, foremost," from root Proto-Indo-European *poti- "powerful; lord." The noun, meaning "that which is possible, anything that may be" is attested by 1817, from the adjective.[1] (Etymonline 2024)

This definition underscores the broad current meaning of "potential," its connections to physics and philosophy, and its dual role as both an adjective and a noun. The term's diverse significances are evident in its synonyms: possibility, potentiality, prospect; promise, capability, capacity, ability, power; aptitude, talent, flair. Conversely, its antonyms—actuality, reality, certainty—highlight the conceptual antithesis of "potential." (Onions 1966, 701)

According to the Collins Dictionary, the synonyms of potential as an adjective are possible, future, likely, promising, budding, embryonic, undeveloped, unrealized, and probable. (Sinclair 2010b) Such synonyms refer to potential as "possible." In addition, synonyms related to this adjective in the sense of "hidden" may be the following: inherent, dormant, latent, possible. Both synonym sets reflect the definition of "potential" as "capable of being or becoming." As a noun, "potential" refers to "a talent not yet in full use": ability, possibilities, capacity, capability, makings, what it takes (informal), aptitude, wherewithal, and potentiality.

Similar definitions and meanings are present in Italian (*potenziale*) and French (*potentialis*) dictionaries. In Italian, the first use was a scientific term in vulgar Latin, as *Potentiale. Di potenzia* comes from Latin *potentialis*. (Nencioni 1987) In French, the first use of the word "potential" was in the field of medicine, and it was then extended to other technical domains.[2] (Bloch 1975) It's noteworthy that the German language offers two distinct translations for "potential." The Latin-derived *Potenzial* (philos., ling.) refers to an unexpressed action, while the Germanic *Leistungsfähigkeit* (phys.) denotes production capacity, productivity, efficiency, and performance. (Meyer and Orlando 1961, 1004)

The etymology of "potential" is widely agreed upon, tracing back to the Latin adjective *potentialis* [-e]. This term, which emerged in the medieval period, is derived from *potens*, meaning "power." What about the meaning of "potential"? While its origins are steeped in philosophical thought, today's usage extends into the scientific realm. Current definitions illustrate this broadening scope, displaying how the term has evolved from its philosophical foundations to encompass a wider, more nuanced significance. Tracing the origins of the concept of potential as a derivation of the word "power," it was observed that the primigenial origin is in the ancient Greek term δυναμις (*dúnamis*), which comes from the verb δύνᾰμαι (*dúnamai*), meaning "I am able to."

Dúnamis is a noun meaning mainly "power" and "capability." Like most ancient Greek terms, it has several meanings according to the context. If this noun refers to a person, it means being powerful/vigorous; if it refers to an object, it assumes the sense of being worthy. It adds to a word the meaning of significance, combines with the verb "to be," δυνατόν ΄στι, *dúnaton esti*, and translates into the impersonal form of "being possible." (Rocci and Argan 2011) The concept of *dúnamis* was used by the ancient Greek philosopher Plato as a general kind of power.[3] Then, in the ninth century B.C., Aristotle defined *dúnamis* as the "principle of change in another or in the thing itself as another," (Zanatta 2009, 1019a, 15–16; 1049b, 5–7) identifying the ancient Greek word with the potential of being; he compared the unactual dimension (*dúnamis)* to the actual form of being.

Since the Middle Ages, the term "potential" had a generic philosophical meaning related to the theological sphere.[4] Nevertheless, other authors (such as Henri Bergson, Gilles Deleuze, and Manuel DeLanda) have explored the concept of potential through post-structural philosophy. (Deleuze and Guattari 1987; Bergson and Mitchell 1911; DeLanda 2002) The contemporary philosopher Françoise Jullien highlighted the potential in Eastern thinking, quoting, among others, Sun-Tzu's writings from the fourth century B.C.. (Jullien 1992; 2002; 2005)

Conceptually, the shift to the hard sciences began with Galileo Galilei's discovery of "gravitational force" in 1638. (Galilei 1638) Isaac Newton's potential theory expanded on Galileo's intuition, providing a mathematical representation of gravitational fields and a precise formula for gravity. (Newton 1686, Annals of Science: 77) The term "potential energy" was first published in 1853 by William Rankine, (Rankine 1853) while the autonomy of the term "potential" from an adjectival to a nominative meaning belonged to Carl Friedrich Gauss' potential function, also called just "potential" in 1839.[5]

Since the 1960s, the concept of "potential" has been widely used to describe human behaviors. It has become shorthand for "human potential" in sociological and pedagogical contexts. However, in everyday usage, the term "potential" functions in two primary ways: as an adjective, meaning "likely to develop into a particular type of person or thing in the future," and as a noun, referring to "the possibility that something will develop in a particular way or have a particular effect." (Murray et al. 1978, vol. 12)

Among its various meanings, the term "potential" is often preceded by a defining word in specialized fields. As highlighted in the survey, the concept of potential is multifaceted. Initially, it is linked to its philosophical origins. It then extends to the notion of potential energy, encompassing a range of specific meanings in mathematics and physics. Additionally, in the social sciences, potential is viewed as a quality or value inherent in humans, both physically and mentally.

Cross-field references on multiple potentials

Philosophy, sciences, and social sciences stand out as the most promising fields for a deeper and more nuanced exploration of the concept of "potential." In philosophy, the concept of potential varies significantly between Eastern and Western approaches. In the Eastern philosophical perspective (in contrast to the Western object-based model), potential and actual are not two distinct levels but two interlaced stages of a process. According to Jullien, the concept of potential itself is related to the scope to be pursued, and exploiting the potential of a situation means making the most of the circumstances for one's own benefit. Indeed, in the Chinese paradigm, a situation or configuration (形 *xing*) develops and takes shape as a relation of forces and the potential (式 *shi*) implied by that situation. (Sun-Tzu and Giles 1910, chap. 5) In Sun Tzu's military treatise from the fourth century B.C., the strategist explained the Eastern concept of *shi* using the images of the mountain stream that drags the stones flowing in it, or the figure of a loaded crossbow that is ready to release its arrow. Assuming that the potential is "determining the circumstances to profit from them," the *xing* and *shi* are part of the same process. (Jullien 2005, 34) The main power embedded in this kind of "situational potential" is its openness, its variability:

> The potential of the situation consists in determining the variable as a function of the profit. You see that this notion of situational potential is thus brought to recover in a positive way, such is its advantage, the notion of "circumstance" on which the European strategy previously stumbled. (Jullien and Lloyd 2004, 16)

In Western philosophy, as mentioned, the concept of potential originates from Aristotelian thought, which reinterprets Plato's dichotomy between unchanging ideas (Forms) and changing physical objects. (Reale 2000) Platonic Forms are abstract, perfect ideals considered more real than the ever-changing physical world. Aristotle, as depicted in Raphael's fresco *The School of Athens*,[6] elevated the realm of reality by introducing the notion of potential, integrating matter and form.[7] In Book V of *Metaphysics*, Aristotle defined potential as something definite, in a definite time and way. He posited that all living things have inherent potentialities that naturally unfold into their appropriate forms, representing their ultimate purpose. Aristotle's notion of *dúnamis* refers to the power to produce change, either as an "active possibility" driving its own evolution or "passive" undergoing transformation. For example, a seed has the potential to become a plant (active), while marble has the potential to be sculpted into a statue (passive).[8]

Turning to contemporary perspectives, Manuel DeLanda frames potential as a "space of possibilities" by introducing the concept of the "virtual." His theory connects Henri Bergson's topological thinking with the spatial theories of Carl Friedrich Gauss and Bernhard Riemann through an interpretation of Deleuzian philosophy. This approach links ontological concepts to scientific theories, where the notion of the "virtual" extends beyond philosophy to encompass physical phenomena. Gilles Deleuze built on Bergson's ideas, integrating them with Riemann's concept of space, where continuous space is influenced by "forces." Bergson's "virtual" is real but not actual. According to DeLanda, the virtual is not an infinite reservoir of "topological essences" (such as attractors) but requires its own form of non-metric temporality. (DeLanda et al. 2005) The potential, as understood through the concept of the "virtual," represents a "space of possibilities" but differs from mere possibility in that it involves actualizable, though not yet realized, potentialities.[9] (DeLanda 2002, 41) This potential as "virtual" is a "quasi-causal" process that emerges from the real. While possibilities are infinite, assuming a virtual space allows for a "tendency" or "structure of possibility," which can be seen as a form of potential. This concept could potentially be applied to architectural materials, advancing and reinterpreting Aristotle's notion of active or passive *dúnamis*.

As Manuel DeLanda's work highlights, the correlation between the concept of potential and hard sciences is significant. In fields like physics and mathematics, potential is used with specific meanings to describe relationships between physical and numerical quantities. These definitions are clearly established with minimal room for interpretation and often become highly specialized. Consequently, the term "potential" has numerous meanings, reflecting over fifty different specializations (Françoise et al. 2006). This discussion focuses on the most relevant types of potential, considering their role in shaping the concept and their intersections with other disciplines.

The Encyclopedia of Mathematical Physics highlights the diverse applications of potential and its evolution. Galileo Galilei's gravitational theory and Isaac Newton's theory of potential established a mathematical framework for gravitational fields, later extended to various other force fields. Initially applied in mechanics (gravitational and Newtonian), the concept has also been utilized in electric and magnetic fields, as well as in biological and chemical contexts. In classic mechanics, Richard Feynman's *Lectures on Physics* discuss potential energy, particularly gravitational potential energy near Earth's surface (Feynman et al. 1963, 4) In mathematics, "potential function" includes various correlation functions, even those outside the strict mathematical definition, such as Green's functions in quantum field theory, which describe "propagators."[10] Between 1813 and 1827, Simeon Poisson and George Green, who coined the term "potential function," established it as a scalar quantity, unlike vector quantities representing both direction and magnitude. While electric potential is the most common form, other types, such as magnetic potential, have been defined for specific purposes. (Besancon 1974, 551)

In classical mechanics, gravitational potential at point B equals the energy transferred, or work per unit mass, to move an object from point A to point B. Similarly, electric potential is analogous to the charge instead of mass. At reference location A, the potential is zero, resulting in negative potential at any finite distance. (ibid.) In physics, fundamental differences in potential depend on the reference system, varying with time, mass (or charge), and position. In mathematics, potential is a function whose mathematical derivative is a physical field, existing as a force or an electric/magnetic field. (Larousse 1971, 16:9782)

The concept of potential in physics and science is functional to give weight to a relationship between position, time, and physical elements.

Relativity and quantum physics offer alternatives to classical mechanics, introducing concepts like gravitational time dilation and the "propagator." Gravitational time dilation occurs when time slows down in stronger gravitational fields. (Bogoliubov 1959, 136–55) The "potential method" in computational complexity theory analyzes amortized time and space complexity of data structures, optimizing operation sequences to reduce infrequent operations' impact. (Cormen et al. 2001)

However, among other fields of science, the notion of potential spans from biology to psychology. In biology, the potential is associated, for instance, with the notion of "resting potential" or, in other words, a difference in electrical potential across the membrane of a cell that is not in the process of transmitting any impulse. (Martin et al. 2008) In this case, the potential underlines a difference between two quantities, a stage of non-equilibrium that means unexploited energy. In evolutionary biology, the concept of potential often refers to a biological system's capacity to adapt. (Darwin et al. 1859) Stephen Gould's "punctuated equilibria" theory describes an organism's ability to rapidly adapt and mutate in response to external changes. Speciation occurs at the edge of a population, where isolation allows for unique adaptations creating survival advantages. (Eldredge and Gould 1971) In this study, the concept of potential emerges within the notion of "exaptation," which relies on the neologism of "pre-adaptation" by Darwin. (Gould and Vrba 1982; Darwin et al. 1859) Pre-adaptation refers to the redundancy between organs and their expected function. This redundancy leaves the possibility of some organs exploiting more than one function along with the biological evolution of the organism. Exaptation refers to traits of biological structures actualized to exploit any different function than the one for which it was originally built, thanks to its original form. This concept suggests that a biological organism has the potential to adapt to unforeseen changes. (Gould and Vrba 1982, 6) In particular, the potential related to an organism's "redundant" features resonates within architecture, potentially applying to objects and buildings as well. Furthermore, the concept of exaptation highlights formal redundancy as a feature that allows for multiple unplanned functions.

In social sciences, the notion of "human potential" has become a central part of the contemporary lexicon, making it the most widespread application of this concept. In psychology, Abraham Maslow's theory of human motivation underlined human needs as a specific force influenced by precise conditions and existing in a "potential" stage. He argued that each person has a hierarchy of needs that is to be satisfied, from basic needs to self-actualization. (Maslow 2013) Several studies focused on the concept of a person's social potential as a complex character of social systems and social dynamics. (Luhmann 1995) However, the philosopher of science and education Israel Scheffler demythologized the classic use of the potential in educational sciences by unfolding three false myths: the myth of fixed potential, the myth of harmonious potentials, and the myth of uniformly valuable potentials. In dismantling these assumptions, he argued that 1) potential is variable, and its variation is never an increase; 2) potentials might be exclusive, not all potential may be developed at the same time; 3) not all potentials are valuable enough to be developed. (Scheffler 1985) Following a similar discourse, the potential might be seen as the possibility to become (that does not need to happen), the capability to become (might become according to the will), or the propensity to become (according to possibility and capability). It is not inherently positive and can be negative, such as the potential to heal or harm.[11]

The Evolution of the
Concept of Potential Across
Time and Disciplines.
Source: Author's Elaboration

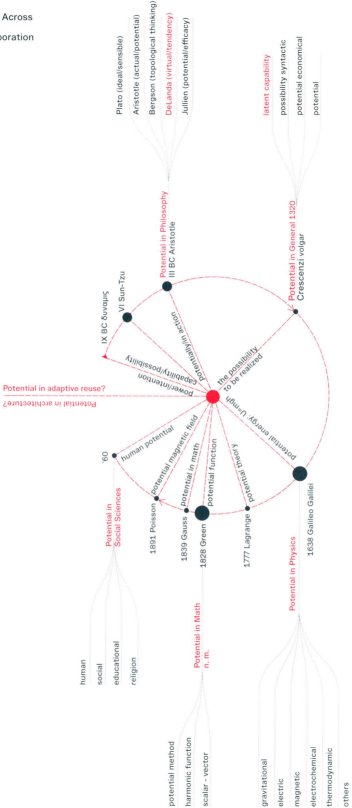

AAA Potential(s)

Features of the concept

The concept of potential weaves through philosophy, hard sciences, and social sciences, uncovering fundamental patterns in its nature. This exploration reveals the cross-features, qualities, and common threads that shed light on how potential can be defined in architecture and adaptive reuse. What about the multiplicity and exclusivity of potential? Despite its widespread use, the concept of potential varies significantly across disciplines, reflecting diverse meanings. Historical and field-specific analyses reveal numerous types of potential. Can we then assert that potential is *inherently multiple*? Furthermore, does the realization of one potential necessarily inhibit the emergence of others? The concept of "multiplicity" in potential involves its varied manifestations depending on initial conditions. This multiplicity includes different types of potential across fields and the interplay between subject and object (i.e., what has potential and for what purpose). Additionally, multiplicity can be understood through a Deleuzian lens of Riemann's space, distinguishing between discrete multiplicity (with its own metrics) and continuous multiplicity (relying on external metrical principles, such as unfolding phenomena or acting forces). (Deleuze 1988, 39)

Indeed, some features embedded in the potential are related to the way of measuring it, by intensive or extensive qualities; for instance, by considering a potential expressed in terms of succession (continuous) or simultaneity (discontinuous or discrete). According to Gilles Deleuze and Félix Guattari's work, the concept itself is more representative of "virtual differences" than of "actual differences" and is evaluated as a continuous system. (Deleuze and Guattari 1987) In physics, potentials are diverse, depending on the force field where they act. They are related not just to quantities (e.g., mass) but also to other action forces (e.g., gravity) and/or space configurations (e.g., distance). Moving to psychology, the existence of various human potentials is a well-known notion. Each human being has various latent potentials to be expressed, and the highest one is self-realization. (Maslow 1943) However, Scheffler dismantled the myth of harmonic potential by arguing that some potentials are mutually exclusive. A person cannot develop all their potential simultaneously, and by choosing one specific potential to develop, they are renouncing to realize other potentials. (Scheffler 1985)

What about the variability and neutrality of potential? The broad meaning of potential could lead to assuming the potential as absolute positive power. However, the "neutrality" of potential emerges in both hard sciences and social studies. In Greek philosophy, the nature of potential is based on transitional stages, from "ideal to real" (Reale 2000) and from "potential to actual." (Zanatta 2009) In Deleuzian philosophy, "variability" is a feature of potential, as a flow of singular transformations. (DeLanda 2002) In Eastern philosophy, the notion of potential is itself linked to a positive meaning, as an efficient systematization of specific circumstances; its positivity is related to achieving a scope (not positive or negative in moral terms), but the fact itself of achieving the result underlies a general positivity of the concept of potential.

The difference among potentials is a fundamental concept in physics, where a state of non-equilibrium causes a change in the energy form in a conservative system. Moreover, in physics, the potential may be either positive or negative. The "sign" depends upon system references and the distance between what is considered the reference and the mass or the charge. (Feynman et al. 1963) The human potential in the educational field is not always positive as it is not always valuable to be realized. In other words, not all potentials have the same value; there exists a hierarchy among them. Moreover, some potentials are even dangerous if realized, as the dismantling of the myth of "uniformly valuable potentials" argues. (Scheffler 1985)

What about the tendency and trigger dependence of potential? In physics, the potential needs a trigger element to be activated. In conservative systems, the potential itself is the ability of the system to release energy, and such potential energy always needs a trigger to be realized. In traditional mechanics, a mass (or a charge in electrics) embeds a potential capable of transforming into kinetic energy, thanks to an applied force that acts as a trigger. Within quantum physics, the propagator, as a function, represents the probability of motion in a given time or, in other words, its tendency to make a specific trajectory. (Besancon 1974; Françoise et al. 2006) Thus emerges a kind of duplicity of possible trends: a tendency that relies on endogenous elements and a trigger that intervenes as an external force and an exogenous influence. Parallelly, among relativistic systems, a trigger dependence between time and potential energy exists, either as a time influence on potential energy or as the variation of this potential as an element influencing the time. This raises a few questions; for instance, does a slow time trigger a high potential, or does a high potential cause a slower speed of time?

In philosophy, following an idealistic perspective, the demiurge transfers ideal qualities to the real world. Such a process is far from the concept of trigger/tendency that emerges in Aristotle. (Duignan 2019) As explored before, "passive potential" requires an external trigger to be transformed (e.g., in the case of the transformation of marble into a sculpture), while "active potential" has an endogenous predisposition to transform (e.g., in the case of transformation of a seed into a plant). Moreover, in post-structuralist philosophy, the tendency is a proper characteristic of the virtual, here considered as potential, where the tendency is a space of possibility, assuming to act into a virtual space and qualifying multiple trajectories of potential. Actualization of potential is itself the expression of a tendency that in an object is related to the actual task that potential aims to perform. Expanding Deleuzian concerns to more complex biological systems, the actualization of a complex process embeds more elaborate energetic possibilities. (Deleuze and Guattari 1987, 214)

In biology, the "punctuated equilibria" evolution theory acts as an extreme case of adaptation. In this context, for example, it discusses what external conditions are relevant in pushing an organism to mutate itself and which process occurs to adapt and to what. It also discusses how much this process is embedded in the physical structure of the organism and how to derive it from exogenous elements. Even if the triggers are still unclear, as argued before, there exists a link between biological evolution, external factors, and time. (Eldredge and Gould 1971) These cross-features—multiplicity and exclusivity, variability and neutrality, tendency and trigger dependence—might offer valuable insights for shaping our understanding of the potential in architecture.

PRECEDENTS FOR THE POTENTIAL IN ARCHITECTURE: LOOKING FOR POTENTIALS

This section acts as a *Wunderkammer*,[12] offering a curated collection of metaphorical, analogical, and direct references to the concept of potential in architecture. It provides a focused yet partial exploration, creating a network of insights that readers can further explore at their own pace.

Metaphorical references to the concept of potential

> We must ask whether the metaphor is an expressive mode with cognitive value. […] We are interested in the metaphor as an additive, not substitutive, instrument of knowledge. (Eco 1984, 89)

Speaking of potential in the context of incompleteness, "incompleteness," or "in-unsettledness," can be defined as an "unsettled shape," "an incomplete virtual state," and an "indeterminate trajectory in accordance with the evolution capacity of a system." (Gausa and Avanzada 2003, 365) We could say that a recognition of any state of incompleteness precedes and triggers a potential for preservation, integration, or demolition. Moreover, the incompleteness can be referred to unrealized (yet or ever) projects to become buildings, (Sky and Stone 1983), unfinished constructions, (Alterazioni Video and Fosbury Architecture 2018) or buildings that achieve incompleteness under decay, catastrophic events, and/or planned deconstruction. (Augé and Serafini 2003; Woodward 2001) The context of incompleteness intertwines with the concepts of "indeterminate" and "eventual loss." In architecture, incompleteness can be an intentional design choice. Take, for instance, Aldo Rossi and Gianni Braghieri's *House of the Dead* in San Cataldo, Modena. The entrance cube resembles a house but is deliberately unfinished—its façades feature regular holes without windows, and it lacks floors and a roof. The building evokes the image of an unfinished and abandoned house, symbolically connecting it to the concept of death. (Rossi 1972, 21)

Yet not all incompleteness is by design. The phenomenon of unfinished buildings, particularly in Europe, often results from financial crises or speculative ventures, leaving behind structures that were never completed or used, forming a landscape of incompleteness. The collective Alterazioni Video has notably explored this in Italy, especially in Sicily, mapping unfinished public works and proposing this "incompleteness" as a new architectural style. They argue that the *Incompiuto* ("unfinished") has become the dominant architectural style in Italy since World War II. This incompleteness opens multiple possibilities—demolition, reconversion, or even the historicization of these structures as a distinct style. The idea that incompleteness, as a style, can open possibilities, is compelling; these buildings, free from functional constraints, resolve the tension between form and purpose. Their lack of purpose transforms them into works of art. (Alterazioni Video and Fosbury Architecture 2018, 17) The authors emphasize the value of preserving and studying unfinished structures, advocating for their "unveiling, temporary activation, reuse, and valorization." (ibid., 11) Similarly, the Spanish Pavilion at the 15th Venice Architecture Biennale explored the theme of "unfinished works" resulting from the 2008 financial crisis. The pavilion underscored the importance of embracing incompletion by rethinking projects as open-ended and adaptable to future needs. The exhibition showcased recent architectural examples shaped by human restraint and economic necessity, designed to evolve with time while celebrating the beauty of age. These projects reflect a vision of architecture as an ever-evolving entity, always in progress and truly serving the needs of people. (Carnicero and Quintáns 2018)

Speaking of potential as indeterminate, we should explore its connection to concepts like vagueness, unfixed states, and unstipulated outcomes. (Sinclair 2010a) The concepts of indeterminate and incomplete architecture often intersect, with indeterminacy adding a distinct layer of meaning to unfinished structures. This exploration began to take shape in the 1960s, as architects experimented with open structural systems that pushed the boundaries of traditional architecture. Cedric Price and Joan Littlewood's *Fun Palace* (1961–64) stands as a milestone in this realm, embodying the essence of indeterminate architecture. Though never built, the *Fun Palace* was envisioned as a flexible, ever-changing space that could adapt to various uses, challenging the notion of a building as a static entity.[13]

In contemporary discussions on indeterminacy and incompleteness, the "Freespace" theme of the 2018 Venice Architecture Biennale highlighted architecture's potential to create spaces that invite interaction and embrace the indeterminate. This approach encourages the design of environments that remain open to change, adaptation, and user engagement, reflecting a shift away from fixed, rigid forms toward more dynamic and evolving spaces. (Farrell and McNamara 2018) This concept celebrated architecture's potential to be adaptable and responsive to the needs of its users, encouraging spaces that evolve over time rather than adhering to fixed, predetermined forms. Similarly, the temporary *Canopy* at MoMA PS1 in New York by nARCHITECTS embodies the concept of the "almost building," characterized by its ephemeral nature and indeterminate boundaries. (Bunge and Hoang 2019, 1) This approach suggests that a state of incompleteness, or indeterminacy, invites engagement, challenging architects to define the minimal level of completeness necessary to establish functional and legible spaces. (ibid., 49) The "almost building" redefines architecture by introducing time as a fourth dimension, questioning whether a building must ever fully reach a stage of completeness.

On the other hand, indeterminacy can also manifest as standardization, where the concept shifts from physical vagueness to a form of efficiency related to the concepts of generic and typical. (Corbellini 2016, 83) This idea, linked to efficiency and uniformity, is evident in Rem Koolhaas's notion of the "Generic City," where urban spaces are designed to meet market demands, devoid of history and uniqueness. (Koolhaas 1995; Koolhaas and Mau 1998, 1250) Koolhaas's perspective is reflected in OMA's *Beijing Preservation* project, where the restoration of the historical hutongs sometimes involves brutal reconstruction, erasing authenticity in favor of a rigid, standardized recreation, ultimately making the past unrecognizable in the name of preservation.

Speaking of potential as a loss, it is clear that we engage with the latent potential embedded in modern and ancient ruins. As Matthew Christopher caught in his powerful images, dismantled buildings—shutdown factories, theatres, hospitals, schools, housing, hotels—have an evocative potential connected to their deterioration, as a physical and abstract incompleteness. (Christopher 2016) Loss is itself connected to decay, obsolescence, and death. As highlighted in the introduction, the concept of loss might reveal a connection with the concept of potential as a metaphor for destructive potential. Perhaps, the attachment to architectural objects increases due to the perception of a forthcoming risk and the fear of losing this object. (Holtorf 2015)

Moreover, if loss is applied to critical heritage discourse, it is considered inevitable and a factor that possibly triggers positive outputs. (DeSilvey and Harrison 2020) Loss is not an ever-desirable condition, but it might be unavoidable and might open novel possibilities in approaching the existing landscape and architecture, especially regarding natural and cultural heritage. With the acceptance of such an ongoing process, we could "open ourselves up to a more meaningful and reciprocal relationship with the material past" (DeSilvey 2017, 179), or even embrace "adaptive release" processes. (DeSilvey et al. 2021)

The proposal for the ruination project of the abandoned St. Peter's Seminary near Glasgow exemplifies the potential inherent in the process of loss. NVA presented an open manifesto for the curated decay of this building, starting in 2018. Although the proposal was never fully realized, it highlighted the concept of conscious partial loss as a form of potential. On the other hand, the anticipation of buildings' afterlife and the consideration of physical deterioration (or even obsolescence) complement the need for reversible and temporally resilient architectures. (Cairns and Jacobs 2014) Considering the loss or, as Cairns and Jacob would say, the death of buildings is a duty of contemporary architecture and, therefore, crucial to delivering sustainable and effective projects. Moreover, a building's lifespan results from accepting inevitable changes in every architectural object, even its physical "death." (ibid., 14) Following this provocative attitude, the act of "discovering the aesthetic potential of waste, of decay, of the inertia of rotten material which serves for no purpose" seems necessary to fit the inevitability of loss and death of anthropic objects (architecture included), people, animals, and plants. (Žižek 2010, 35) This kind of potential, embedded in loss, inspired heritage practice to work with (rather than against) transience and decay within a transient ecology framework. (DeSilvey and Harrison 2020) Following the post-preservationist discourse, loss is a metaphor for destructive potential, as a process that is embedded in life and affected by natural disasters, climate change, and abandonment. (DeSilvey 2017) By exploring the stages and circumstances where it occurs, it is possible to observe and even appreciate this loss process, led by non-human agents or palliative interventions, as Caitlin DeSilvey explored, or the activation of other forms and kinds of memory, not linked to the physical conservation of a well-established category of heritage. (Holtorf 2015) On the other hand, when considering the process of loss and change as a crucial part of life and concurring to set and increase our perception of heritage value, it is not the loss that is problematic but how individuals, communities, and societies deal with it. For example, in Eastern tradition, temples are demolished and rebuilt every 20 years, and it represents a memory-making process. (Fluck and Wiggins 2017) Loss plays with impermanence too. *Architecture must burn* explores "blurred" and "translucent" spaces, in both physical (urban sprawls and material qualities) and conceptual (indeterminacy, uncertainty) terms. In these terms, architecture might become ephemeral and not permanent. (Betsky and Adigard 2000)

Indirect references to the concept of potential

"Analogy is a cognitive mechanism that allows us to transfer knowledge from one domain to another by recognizing structural similarities between them. It operates through a process of mapping correspondences from a familiar domain (the source) to an unfamiliar one (the target), enabling new insights and understanding." (Eco 1979, 42)

Analogy explores terms and concepts akin to potential—such as "chance," "latency," and "capability (to change)"—each embodying distinct nuances of potential.

First analogy: the concept of "chance." Chance is literally "an occasion that allows something to be done." It is synonymous with possibility (and potential). (Cambridge University 2024a) While change is often seen as a positive force, it can also be viewed through a more critical lens in architectural thinking. In Leon Battista Alberti's *De re aedificatoria*, chance is regarded as a negative element that architects should strive to avoid. Alberti advocates for complete control over architectural design, emphasizing the importance of meticulous planning to prevent the need for revisions and alterations once construction has begun. (Alberti et al. 1966, IX.9) This dichotomy between "the result of necessity" and chance is embedded in architectural practice, not as an opposition to design but as an integral part of every project. Chance, with its various nuances, is a constant presence in architectural design. As Yeoryia Manolopoulou (2013) suggests, the "chance factor" functions as a structure of coincidence where synchronicity plays a crucial role. This simultaneity in chance contributes to the creation of spatiality, making it an essential aspect of the architectural experience. (Manolopoulou 2007) Engaging with chance can take five forms: impulsive chance, driven by intuition and imagination; systematic chance, which uses methodical approaches to generate variability; fabricated chance, based on rational and statistical methods; active chance, involving collaborative, open-ended creation; and resistant chance, which accepts chance as an inevitable factor influencing outcomes and conceiving "the building as an autonomous object, recognizing that it will inevitably be complemented by chance as its other." (Manolopoulou 2013, xxiii) Therefore, accepting chance means recognizing a lack of control in architectural design and construction by accepting the contextual influence, the agents' actions, and the sum of all unexpected and uncontrolled conditions that might occur. On the other hand, the so-called systematic chance is not perceived as lawless chaos but as a rule, embedded in nature, and the universe might drive a probabilistic and rational application of this concept. (Hacking 1990)

In contemporary architecture, Coop Himmelb(l)au showcase buildings as active participants in a universal energy balance, integrating natural forces such as sun, wind, water, and vegetation to create self-sustaining structures. Wolf D. Prix and his team use parametric design to develop an architecture that is intentionally dynamic and responsive to various agents of change. This approach is evident in both large-scale projects, like the Museum of Confluences in Lyon, and smaller interventions, such as the rooftop remodeling on Falkestrasse in Vienna.[14]

Second analogy: the concept of "latency." Latency means "the fact of being present but needing particular conditions to become active, obvious, or completely developed." (Cambridge University 2024c) Considering latency as analogous to potential, it is related to present qualities embedded in the building as an implicit value of construction. Stemming from the roots of architectural manuals, the idea of implied qualities that existing constructions have (or are likely to have) is widely present in Vitruvius's ten books of architecture. (Pollio and Gwilt 1874) In particular, this latency might be expressed in terms of *firmitas*, *utilitas*, and *venustas*, encompassing matter, function, and appearance, respectively.[15] *Firmitas* means solidity and strength in structure and material and includes the concept of durability; *utilitas* concerns the practical utility and functional use of constructions; and *venustas* is the beauty concerning the appearance of the architecture. On the other hand, for Alberti, *venustas* is the most crucial trait in architecture—"the noblest and most necessary of all." (Heath 1989; van Eck 1998) According to Vitruvius, form and function are latent qualities awaiting realization through an architectural project. This concept of functional utility is present in Riegl's "theory of values." In his framework, among various values, use-value pertains to the intended function of a monument. (Riegl 1984)

A wide number of projects dealing with the power of circumstance, the site setting, and the context would require an extensive analysis to be presented. For instance, Giorgio Grassi's restoration project for the ancient theater in Sagunto unlocks the latent potential of the building's material integrity. His focus is on completing the Roman theater's structures, which are crucial for its identification as such, including the reconstruction of the *summa cavea*. This project underscores how potential extends beyond just the built environment to encompass site conditions as well. The importance of site—viewed as a "circumstance already in place, waiting to be developed"—echoes themes in Eastern philosophical thought. Latency is reflected in concepts such as "spirit of place" or "atmosphere." *Genius loci*, rooted in Roman mythology[16] and explored by Christian Norberg-Schulz, highlights how a place's inherent qualities must be preserved and activated in architectural design. Norberg-Schulz advocates for a phenomenology of architecture that respects the latent features, values, and natural qualities intrinsic to a location. (Norberg-Schulz 1980, 4) This latent capability concerns the concept of place as a "psychic function" that depends on identification, implying a sense of belonging. (ibid., 166)

A different concept of the latent power of a place emerged in Aldo Rossi's work as a theory of *locus*. He states that the pre-existence is manifested through the permanence of the tracks, from the position, which characterizes the axes of settlement development. (Rossi 1966) He empathizes how "the city is born in a place, but it is the street that keeps it alive." In case these signs get lost, the *locus* remains, as the site, the place, and a non-removable form. (Rossi 1981, 43)

The qualities of many buildings are deeply rooted in the morphology and nature of their environmental context, construction materials, and structural integrity. Beyond these, both tangible and intangible factors contribute to defining the character of a place—latent aspects that architects must consider in their designs.[17]

Third analogy: the concept of "capability to change." A striking example of potential as a tangible force is found in the work of Lancelot "Capability" Brown, one of the most influential landscape designers of the eighteenth century. Brown earned his nickname by analyzing and maximizing the potential of a site's conditions, skillfully manipulating topography to create naturalistic landscapes. He employed elements like turf, still water mirrors, and carefully arranged trees in clumps or loose belts, without relying on carved stone or architectural forms.[18] This approach to mapping and re-making landscapes to continuously unfold their potential and reveal diverse features resonates with contemporary mapping theory. (Corner 2002, 213–300)

Shifting from landscape to buildings, the literature focused on responsive components addresses the idea of potential as "capability to change" through demolition and disassembly. This potential as part of the design process is widely present in the narrative related to flexibility within the current architectural design debate. Therefore, the capability to change might be intended as flexibility—the "capacity of a building to absorb minor and major change." (Grammenos and Russell 1997) In architecture, the work of John Habraken recognized the "capability to change" as a crucial dynamic, emphasizing its importance in his "Supports/Infill" theory.[19] This theory distinguishes between fixed structural elements (support) and adaptable components (infill), giving users the possibility to personalize their living spaces while sharing common infrastructure, empowering individuals to make decisions about their own environments. (Habraken 1991) Stephen Kendall's extended work on the *Open Building* projects further demonstrates the practical application of this concept, showcasing its ongoing relevance and evolution in architectural practice. (Kendall 1999)

"Design for flexibility" means manipulating design factors affecting a construction's adaptability to increase it. (Gosling et al. 2013) In this case, adaptability is the ability to respond to environmental uncertainty while the type of change is unknown at the time of design and construction. (van Ellen et al. 2021) Umberto Eco focused explicitly on understanding what it means for an author to consciously accept and pursue a work as open to change. This contribution raises a significant question for all creative practices, including architecture. (Eco 1962) The Faculty of Architecture in Caracas, designed by Carlos Raul Villanueva, is an example of openwork. In particular, this building is defined as an example of architecture in motion, capable of continuously reinventing itself. For example, the classrooms are built using mobile panels to allow users to build a study environment that meets their specific needs by changing the layout and morphology of the rooms when required. (ibid., 43)

Hughes and Sadler proposed the "open to change" as "unstructured," critically editing various essays on "freedom participation and change in modern and contemporary architecture panorama." (Hughes and Sadler 2000) In particular, Hughes quotes the strategy of "indeterminacy" by Weeks, opening up the connection between the "uncertainty principle" in quantum mechanics and the design of hospital buildings. (Huges 2000) Weeks challenged the fixity of dimension for hospitals by proposing a series of departments with no fixed lengths for the Northwick Park Hospital, that is, a structure free from internal walls and modular systems. (Week 1966) Instead, these buildings have "extendable ends" (made of easily removable steel panels).[20] (Hughes and Sadler 2000, 97–98) What should we expect to be a matter of change in a building then? Sara Slaughter argued that three general types of changes can be expected to occur in space: changes in the function of space, changes in the load carried by the building, and changes in the flux of people and forces from the environment. (Slaughter 2001)

> Direct references to the potential in architecture
> and adaptive reuse

How has the concept of potential been explicitly woven into the fabric of architectural discourse?

Shifting from landscape to buildings, the potential has been acknowledged as related to materials, and building technology appears in the third chapter of Sigfried Gideon's book "Space, time and architecture." Gideon focused on "the evolution of new potentialities" while exploring the process of industrialization of construction and the structural system evolution during the modern age. (Giedion 1982) Furthermore, he generally argued that potentialities are stored in historical models, and thanks to critical analysis, architects can unfold them to innovate and create a change in tradition. In particular, Gideon underlined the potentialities related to filling the gap between history and architectural activity. (Giedion 1954, 8, 19)

These ideas greatly influenced Manfredo Tafuri's concept of "operative criticism" in architectural history. Tafuri viewed potential as an inherent force in the analysis of architecture and art, arguing that any critical examination must integrate a "potential tendency" that directs exploration with a clear focus on historical and political objectives. (Tafuri 1980, 141) This notion of tendency acts as a crucial link between the past and the future, bridging current conditions with future aspirations—a connection that is deeply rooted in the concept of potential itself. But how does this connection manifest? In the 1980s, Aldo Rossi offered a compelling example of potential energy in architecture, describing it as an anticipatory force—an energy intrinsically linked to matter and transformation. (Rossi 1981)

> The mason was struck by the fact that expended energy does not get lost; it remains stored for many years, never diminished, latent in the block of stone, until one day it happens that the block slides off the roof and falls on the head of a passerby, killing him. [...] In architecture this search is also undoubtedly bound up with the material and with energy; and if one fails to take note of this, it is not possible to comprehend any building, either from a technical point of view or from a compositional one. In the use of every material, there must be an anticipation of the construction of a place and its transformation. (ibid., 1)

Aldo Rossi relies on physicist Max Planck's account of a "schoolmaster's story" about a mason who heaved a block of stone up on the roof of a house with great effort. We might consider that this interpretation of potential contrasts with Rem Koolhaas's view, where the potential is seen as a kind of absence of architecture itself.[21] In contrast, Aldo Rossi's perspective sees potential embodied in material constraints, defining architecture through its unique, locally grounded interactions. This interpretation highlights how potential in architecture isn't just about what is but what could be, encapsulating the dynamic interplay between form, function, and future possibilities. (Reiser and Umemoto 2006, 21–23)

> We assert the primacy of material and formal specificity over myth and interpretation. In fact, while all myths and interpretations are derived from the immediacy of material phenomena, this equation is not reversible. When you try to make fact out of myth, language only begets more language, with architecture assuming the role of illustration or allegory. This is true not only of the initial condition of architecture but actually plays out during the design process in a similar way. Material practice is the shift from asking "what does this mean?" to "what does this do?" (ibid., 23)

In this context, potential becomes the bridge between ideal and material practice in architecture. It brings to light how potential isn't merely a theoretical concept but a tangible force that manifests in the physical abilities of architecture—whether it's bearing weight, creating an atmosphere, or defining a space.

Goethe's concept of the archetypal plant (*Urpflanze*)[22] serves as a powerful metaphor for exploring morphological variations and potential. This idea illustrates how potential unfolds through the plant's evolutionary stages, from seed formation to flowering and fruiting, with each phase offering a snapshot of its dynamic progression over time. The plant's growth and transformations reflect its inherent potential and adaptability. Jesse Reiser and Nanako Umemoto in their provocative *Atlas of Novel Tectonics* draw a parallel between these natural variations and architectural forms, adopting an essentialist perspective rather than an idealistic one. They suggest that, much like Goethe's archetypal plant, architectural forms are defined in terms of

Goethe's archetypal plant, with key features outlined as potentials. Redrawn by the author, based on (Reiser and Umemoto, 2007, 63)

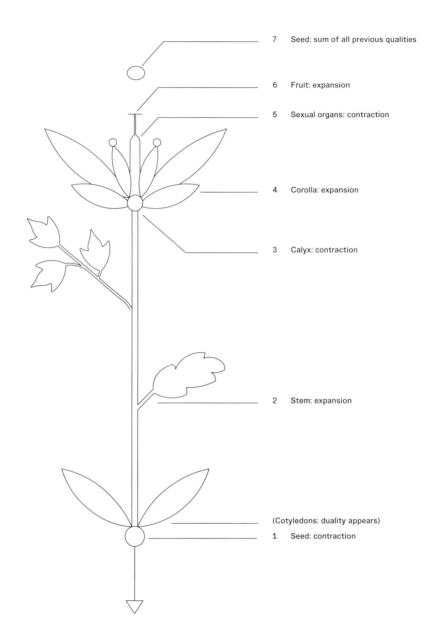

Precedents for the potential in architecture: looking for potentials

potential by their evolving nature, highlighting how potential is realized through continuous change rather than fixed ideals.

Moreover, the discourse on adaptive reuse and preservation theory extensively employs the concept of potential, using various terms such as "potential for development and innovation," "adaptation potential," "untapped potential," "new growth potential," "tectonic potential," "negative potential," and "self-destructive potential." These terms illustrate the multifaceted application of potential in both heritage and urban legacy contexts. For heritage buildings, Bie Plevoets and Koenraad Van Cleempoel emphasize the importance of "activating the full potential" of monuments and sites under preservation, viewing this as a central challenge in adaptive reuse.

> The potential of adaptive reuse as a way to regenerate heritage buildings and sites and historic urban and rural areas is also recognized in the field of conservation. [...] Rather than freezing a building's historic fabric, this complex task seeks to activate the full potential of its heritage and draws on the ambitious idea that the heyday of a monument or site may also lay in the future. (Plevoets and Van Cleempoel 2019, 109–236)

By doing this, they recognized the adaptive reuse as part of "the field of conservation," the adaptive reuse as a potential and, especially, the existence of a potential to be activated through a design project; such activation of potential is a complex but fundamental objective in adaptive reuse. (ibid.) In the realm of architectural manuals, James Douglas's *Building Adaptations* provides a simple but compelling take on the concept of potential. Far from being merely a metric for gauging a building's adaptability, Douglas offers a nuanced definition. He characterizes "building adaptation potential" as a blend of multiple factors: location, condition, construction, morphology, and legal constraints. Together, these elements shape the extent to which a building can evolve and adapt through reuse. (Douglas 2006, 62–63)

> The shape and height of the building will have a bearing on its ability to accommodate modifications to its interior and exterior. Rectangular or square buildings are much easier to facilitate an extension or other external alteration. Internally, too, these layouts can be more conveniently reconfigured. Circular, curved or irregular shaped buildings, on the other hand, are more awkward and thus more expensive to adapt. [...] This [adaptation potential] relates to the alternative use and layout of the existing building. The property's location, condition, construction, morphology, and legal restraints will all influence the degree to which it can be adapted. (Douglas 2006, 62)

In particular, "layout and configuration" play a crucial role in assessing a "building's adaptation potential," where a building's adaptation is "any work to a building over and above maintenance to change its capacity, function or performance when considered obsolete." (Douglas 2006, 1) Here, a holistic approach emerges due to the need to frame an overall degree of unexpressed adaptability in practical terms. However, it is possible to argue that some of these variables are more fixed than others. For instance, a legal restraint might change due to time, while morphology, construction technology, and site location cannot change. Following an analogous discourse, Stewart Brand divided buildings into five "shearing layers of change": site, structure, skin, services, and space plan. (Brand 1995) Among these, the site is eternal. After the site comes the structure that "persists and dominates." The structure is then followed by skin, which is mutable; interiors (space plan), which might change radically, and stuff, which can "just keep moving." (Brand 1995, 18)

Moreover, the "new growth potential" refers to an intervention that prefigures a potential addition in height or eventual space to be extended in its planimetric distribution. (White 1999) In other words, this potential is based on the open possibilities embedded in an unbuilt plot, a void in the urban fabric.[23] In the book *Du potential des grandes structures Urbaine abandonnées*, architecture, abandonment, and potential are presented as "three terms for a fertile equation." (Chupin and Abenia 2017, 13) Here, the term "potential" mediates the relationship between architecture and abandonment, outlining the relation of abandonment to unrealized, unfinished, and dismissed architecture. In particular, the book includes the following two categories: abandonment occurring during the construction stage or after the first-use phase. Resistance and potential are considered as counterparts in the design adaptation of abandoned large structures. Besides, the differences between resistance and potential intend to identify the conditions that "enable a project to emerge within an abandoned large urban structure." (Chupin and Abenia 2017, 15) The paradigmatic case is presented in *Silo No. 5* in Montreal, following the perspective of several attempted projects. In addition, Louis Destombes highlighted the "potential *tectonique*" particularly visible during the construction phase and in the ruin stage. (Chupin and Abenia 2017, 24–25) In the end, some features of potential in large abandoned urban structures emerge. First, the potential exists related to a "suspended stage." Second, it might be expressed in the form of a gradient. Third, the tension between resistance and gradients of potential expresses the survival of large abandoned urban structures. A tension exists between resistance and potential, and this tension allows us to determine a "tendency" in adaptation. For example, demolition is likely to occur in the case of a large structure with a weak resistance and a weak potential. On the contrary, cases with high potential and high resistance are challenging when it comes to allowing any interventions (demolition/reuse/planned abandoning). Indeed, Tiphaine Abeina deemed it urgent to consider the "problematic cases" where buildings have high potential and high resistance. (Abenia 2017)

In the realm of industrial adaptive reuse, the concept of potential has been explored in varied and thought-provoking ways. Matteo Robiglio's *Toolkit for Post-Industrial Cities* provides a foundation for integrating the idea of potential with embodied energy—described as the energy initially invested in producing and assembling building components. This energy remains embedded in the structure, even as its original functions become obsolete. (Robiglio 2017, 198) Such overall potential is in part composed of energy stored in dismissed buildings and in part related to the new possibilities that these "ruins" prefigure. In addition, the potential is affected by social, economic, and legal constraints. Such a potential awaits to be activated through design intervention. (Robiglio 2017, 198–203)

> In heritage preservation, locality is inherited, not produced, and has to be preserved. In adaptive reuse, *the potential of legacy* has to be activated in order to produce a new form of locality. (ibid., 203)

However, activating this dormant potential requires an assessment of it in the first place.[24] This particular potential to be maximized emerges as related to the structural system, the morphology of space, the dimensions and the volumetric extensions of the construction. (ibid., 151–52) Such a dormant potential is untangled as a not-always-positive matter. In fact, "potential can also be negative and even turn into a hazard," for instance, in the case of polluted sites, which often require unsustainable costs. (ibid., 152) Other references to the concept of potential emerge following the premise of this research: to expand adaptive reuse boundaries by including "Postpreservation" and "Counterpreservation" as practices interlaced with adaptive reuse. (DeSilvey 2017, 13–15) Thus, the first crucial contribution is nested within the concept of "Counterpreservation" coined by Daniela Sandler. (Sandler 2016). She highlighted the idea of self-destructive potential as a transformative and dynamic change of things (buildings):

> The *self-destructive potential* of Counterpreservation is inseparable from the idea of growth, life, and construction. One way to understand this paradox may be to focus on the process of change, that is, the idea of transformation and dynamism, instead of fixating the analysis on the end result of this process, that is, extinction. [...] If we were to understand transformation merely in terms of destruction, this would mean focusing only on what is lost in the process instead of embracing the new. (ibid., 235–36)

This kind of potential is strictly related to how people choose to deal with a building's decay. Thus, people embrace a "counterpreservative approach" as an act of resistance and cultural appropriation. On the other hand, in the post-preservationist approach, Caitlin DeSilvey referred to the potential as entropy:

> An *entropic approach* makes emerge a potential to unfold along multiple trajectories; what may appear to erasure on one register may be generative of new information on another. [...] It may be that in some circumstances a state of gradual decay provides more opportunities for memory-making and more potential points of engagement and interpretation than the alternative. (DeSilvey 2017, 13–15)

Interlacing entropy with potential means accepting that loss is a part of the potential.[25] Within the contemporary architectural debate, Koolhaas has considered universal urbanism as territories with potential in a systemic process. (Koolhaas and Mau 1998, 969) Nevertheless, the provocative vision that Koolhaas presented in the "Cronocaos" exhibition at the Venice Biennale in 2010 particularly highlights the high transformation (or demolition) potential that exists in the built environment under preservation.[26] Therefore, the increase in highly preserved building stock represents the leading phenomenon of contemporary architecture. Koolhaas proposed the development of a counter-theory of preservation that defines what should be demolished rather than conserved. (OMA and Koolhaas 2011) OMA's preservation manifesto, "reconstructed from fragmentary evidence by Jorge Otero-Pailos," states that preservation has the potential to be an "architecture's formless substitution." (Koolhaas et al. 2014)

Can we speak of transformative potential, then? The potential linked to transformation across time and due to a design intervention represents the focus of this book. Nevertheless, this semantic instability of what might be considered potential is the quintessence of several theoretical problems that architecture has to deal with due to the complexity of architectural design: which materials, how in terms of form and shape, and for whom. As seen before, preservation is the main field of research where the architectural project's interpretative nature can define the undefinable by means of other methodologies. According to the Cambridge dictionary, the word "transformative" means "causing a major change to something or someone, especially in a way that makes it or them better." (Cambridge University 2024d) It does not necessarily refer to "major changes" within the field of adaptive reuse, the past has been adapted either by slight modifications or major interventions. Back in 1997, the idea of "transformative architecture" yet encompassed conservation, adaptations, and renovations in existing buildings either by slight modifications or major interventions.[27]

On the other hand, the metaphorical references to the terms "incompleteness," "indeterminate," and "loss" and the analogical references to "chance," "latency," and "capability (to change)" represent a transversal level of reading. Such layering highlights the theoretical facets that the potential embeds. As Noam Chomsky's theory introduces, there exists an initial state where a speaker pronounces the first word, and then she/he passes to a second state where the choice of the second word is limited, and each state through which the speaker passes embeds grammatical restrictions exponentially limiting the choices of words. (Chomsky 1965) Therefore, the simplest type of grammar can generate an infinite number of sentences with a finite apparatus—whereby "infinite" refers to a number almost infinite as reality but potentially infinite as a possibility. This pattern of reduction of options embeds a transformative tendency, here called *transformative potential*. As in the transformative lexicon, existing buildings might be perceived in terms of transformative options, where there is a "deep structure" and a "surface structure," the former being the subject of obligatory transformations and the latter being "optional transformation." Direct references concerning the potential as a "physical capability of architecture to do" have emerged in a contemporary shift from the ideal to a material practice of architecture. (Reiser and Umemoto 2006) In terms of morphological changes, an organism (buildings included) shall be considered both in morphology and material consistency. A potential is stored in construction materials as stagnant energy. (Rossi 1981) Moreover, existing potentialities are used to define the design outcome. Finally, these potentials are linked to environmental and landscape conditions and the model of questioning the landscape.

Furthermore, potential as a possibility has emerged thanks to technological development in society. Besides, thinking in terms of potential implies structuring architectural exploration toward a particular target. However, a shared feature among these references lies in the dynamics of mutation, change, and adaptation within architecture; these dynamics involve theory, design, and analysis. Indeed, within the adaptive reuse theory, the potential is a matter of interest in the adaptive reuse of heritage buildings. (Plevoets and Van Cleempoel 2019) The "adaptation's potential" concerns dimensions, morphology, construction, location, decay condition, and legal restraints. (Douglas 2006) Besides, time plays a relevant role, affecting the deterioration of building elements and ageing at different paces according to fixity. (Brand 1995) The "new growth potential" is also the physical expandability of an existing building. (White 1999) Moreover, the potential is expressed in gradients, ranking the tendency of buildings to be demolished or adapted according to the "resistance" (structurally and constructively) that makes it last. (Chupin and Abenia 2017) Furthermore, the potential is manifold, in part composed of the energy embedded in materials in place and its possibilities to be activated (particularly in the case of non-heritage buildings). Among the various kinds of potential*s*, negative potential*s* exist. Some potentials are maximizable through the design project: structural system, morphology, volumetric asset. (Douglas 2006; Robiglio 2017) Moreover, by embracing an overlap with adaptive reuse from "counterpreservation" and "post-preservation" theories. A self-destructive potential (Sandler 2016) and an entropic potential (Desilvey 2017) open the possibility of considering a conscious loss and destruction as a form of adaptation that might occur. A strategy fostering a planned demolition due to the rising invasive "extreme preservation" might open possibilities to the untapped potential embedded in the existing building stock. (Koolhaas 2011; Koolhaas et al. 2014) In conclusion, potential cannot be defined in isolation; it is an inherently multidisciplinary concept with a rich, multifaceted significance in architecture. Its meaning remains elusive, especially within adaptive reuse, where its definitions and applications are equally complex and nuanced.

A TRANSFORMATIVE POTENTIAL OF FORM: TOWARD A NEW METHODOLOGY

The architectural history of obsolescence teaches us about polytemporality. We live in an age of both obsolescence and sustainability, past and present all at once. Yet polytemporality is not a full theory of time. It is a static snapshot describing a single moment's complexity that implicitly suggests a process of cumulative change rather than rupture, the past continuing into the present. But this does not account for how change happens… (Abramson 2016, 148)

The actions of time on transformation

Kronos or Kairos? To understand buildings' change, Gavin Lucas proposes looking at buildings through the notion of persistence. From an archaeological perspective, a building changes not only over a long period but also requires analysis due to the rate of change of singular elements, each with its own "rhythm, tempos, speed." (Lucas 2012; Bille and Sorensen 2016, 51) To outline this ambivalence of the concept of time, the ancient Greek terms *Kairos* (καιρός) and *Kronos* (χρόνος) can support the exploration of two diverse types of time or two different perceptions of the phenomena within time. In the ancient Greek language, there is *Kronos*, a linear, quantitative time, and *Kairos*, a qualitative time that symbolizes the opportune moment when something specific might happen. (Smith 1969) This dual pace of time is present in the thoughts of Walter Benjamin and Friedrich Nietzsche. *Kairos* is present both in Nietzsche's "tragic time" and Benjamin's "time for revolution." (Gurisatti 2019) While Benjamin presents *Kairos* as the "time to act," the shearing time, close to the linear or circular time (*Kronos*), Nietzsche explores *Kairos* as the moment when the chain of time breaks, and the fragments then have the chance to reassemble in novel configurations due to the unexpected event, the emergency time. (ibid., 66) Moreover, in terms of the "right moment," *Kairos* might embed "perishability" as the "instant of acceptance of decay." (Barthes 2019, 42) Finally, in terms of "neutral," *Kairos* recognizes the rightness of a process, even accepting its fragility and contingency. (Barthes 2002) The relation between form and time (buildings in terms of form and buildings in terms of process) and their mutual influence re-marks the continuous change of forms, rapid or slow, while process "is inherently temporal in its passing and planning of form." In other words, form and process are strictly connected rather than in opposition. (Bille and Sorensen 2016, 50) Still, there exists a kind of "break-even point," a turning point where something happens; when the building is not considered a building anymore, but a ruin or a trace of what was once a building. (Brand 1995, 112)

Ruins or rust? Speaking of ruins, there is a long tradition of thoughts by several authors. As Georg Simmel writes in his book *Die Ruine*, ruins represent a stage "between the not-yet and the no–longer," where forces of nature balance a decline of human forces, opening up fascinations to incompleteness. (Simmel 1919, 125–133) However, a shift from the idea that ruin pertains solely to monumental objects is outlined by Woodward, who recognizes a broader interest in ruins over their monumentality. (Woodward 2001, 34) To do so, he challenges the notion of *Ruinenwert* (ruin value) by Speer. The ruin as a symbolic form related to the power of civilization was not by chance introduced by Albert Speer during the Nazi regime to validate ideological identitarian means in the stones of buildings. The relationship between totalitarian regimes and ruins will require a study of its own, but it is necessary here to understand the symbolic charge of the ruin and its potential, even when unrelated to any use. During the Nazi regime, due to this concept of "ruin value," it was forbidden to use steel and iron-concrete constructions in administrative public buildings because of their higher susceptibility to deterioration. On the contrary, Woodward proposes to explore ruins through the lens of incompleteness rather than monumentality: "Poets and painters like ruins, and dictators like monuments." (ibid.) In dealing with them, embracing deterioration is not a new idea; back in the nineteenth century, John Ruskin saw memory as a pillar of architecture alongside tradition and truth. A human being recognizes the past through architecture, and time emerges as a critical in-state, "the glory of a building is in its age." (Ruskin 1849, 195) In his essay "Architecture in ruins," Jonathan Hill explores the approaches to ruins across history, outlining, among others, Piranesi's drawings as a "creation of ruins" and Louis Kahn's conception of ruins as either a potential or a "shame." (Hill 2019) As Louis Kahn underlines, decay may open up freedom to intervene in an existing structure. (Latour 1991) Considering a ruin as "a metaphor of passage of time, inevitable decay and potential renewal" might open up multiple suggestions on an eventual renewal (or not). (Hill 2019, 102)

However, ruin and rust are different kinds of remains both representative of the passage of time on an architectural object. Ruins, as commonly mentioned, could be perceived as a trace of the past overtaken by nature, while rust, in terms of post-industrial traces, is a recent (painful) reminder of loss. (Picon 2000)

"Rust" is defined as a product of industrial society, while ruin pertains to a craftsman's age. The redundancy of mass-production architecture (as industrial factories) and the obsolescence of this architecture are elements that emerge to support this distinction. (Picon 2000) Besides, a "skeletal architecture," as Bernard Rudofsky remarks while presenting a rustic conservatory stripped of roofs and walls on Lake Garda, is considered a ruin or rust. Here, the difference between the two concepts is related to the significance of relying on the human perception of the fragments. (Rudofsky 1987, 112)

In adaptive reuse practice, ruin and rust are overlapping concepts while adapting existing yet partial structures. According to Douglas, a "ruinous" building is rated as "Bad" (the lowest level in the four-grade scale). In this case, only some walls are left, with little or no roof structure remaining, no windows and doors remaining intact, and the building is often classed as a "wreck." (Douglas 2006, 71) On the other hand, the range of possible adaptation includes "restoration, conservation, conversion to other uses."[28] As for ruins, the transformative potentials seem more related to their process of controlled deterioration and the eventual friction between any attempt to complete them through an architectural project. Whereas speaking of "rust" has the potential to be consciously destroyed or totally transformed.

Physical deterioration and obsolescence? Deterioration is constant and concerns the physical elements of each building. (Brand 1995, 112) Whereas obsolescence has been defined as a sum of many kinds of obsolesce: physical, economic, financial, functional, locational, environmental, political, market, style, and control obsolescence. The criteria to define these sub-types of obsolescence are related to a specific causal factor and subsequent fixes. (Butt et al. 2015) Obsolescence can be considered as a sum of functional, "relative," and "absolute" obsolescence concerning the building itself and its location. (Buitelaar et al. 2021, 2) Relative building obsolescence occurs when the current use is no longer the "highest and best use." Then, there may be a loss of capital appreciation since there is a higher-value use available. Besides, "absolute obsolescence (or deterioration) becomes visible through the physical appearance, specifically the level of maintenance." Therefore, obsolescence has been framed as an unavoidable urban, dynamic process that requires an anticipatory intervention to be fixed, especially in terms of urban policy. (ibid., 3–6) Obsolescence could be represented as an "inexorable process of devaluation" and "this decline arrested just temporarily by rebuilding or adaptation."[29] (Abramson 2016, 73) Abramson retraces three main approaches in fixing obsolescence: making sure that a building may work regardless of functional change, stabilizing architectural form against architectural deformation, or picturing the process of obsolescence and embracing it. (ibid., 79) The inevitability of obsolescence is widely recognized and explored with flexible and short-life design solutions. On the other hand, other architects tried to resist obsolescence through preservation and adaptive reuse. According to Daniel Abramson, buildings have a finite life, and obsolescence acts as a metric between time and substance.

However, obsolescence was invented in the late 1800s, while deterioration and decay has existed throughout history as the physical impact of time or external agents on objects. (ibid., 12–16)

Deterioration, as "decay beyond normal repair," is something that can be controlled and is a continuous process, therefore it is predictable. Moreover, it is a physical condition that could be contrasted through maintenance, repair and renovation, renewal, modernization, or retrofitting. (Douglas 2006, 28) Deterioration—or absolute obsolescence—is a natural condition that tends to happen in the absence of any opposing force. In other words, there exists "a tendency for things to drift in the direction of greater disorder or greater entropy." (ibid., 28) In buildings, decay might anticipate death or be evidence that death already occurred in functional terms. Deterioration is visible in the patina, dirt, rust, bio-receptivity, and weathering. (Cairns and Jacobs 2014, 69–100) This phenomenon of physical decay encompasses ruins, monuments, rust, and dross, outlining positive or negative outputs.[30] According to Brand, deterioration affects all buildings regardless of their construction time. (Brand 1995, 112)

How to assess the impact of time in adaptive reuse then? Stewart Brand's shearing layers highlight the different rates of change of building components, integrating the theme of rates of change and diverse timing into a change of the components that articulate a building as a system. (ibid., 13) He builds upon the foundation established by Francis Duffy, who examined the rates of change in office interiors for the RIBA. (Duffy 1992) In particular, the concept of "shearing layers of change" categorizes a building into distinct layers—six "S"—based on their lifespan. His works rely on Francis Duffy's five layers of change: the "Site"—the geographical setting—is considered eternal; the "Structure"—including foundations and load-bearing elements—lasts up to 300 years; the "Skin"—the exterior surfaces—changes every 20 years; "Services"—such as electrical wiring, plumbing, HVAC, and elevators—typically last 7 to 15 years; the "Space plan"—the interior layout, including walls, ceilings, floors, and doors—varies between every 1 to 30 years; and "Stuff"—furniture—changes continuously.[31] (Brand 1995, 14–17) Additionally, Bernard Leupen introduces a sixth layer, "Access," which encompasses the circulation system. This layer influences the adaptability of the space it creates. (Leupen 2006) In their evaluation of heritage buildings, Marieke Kuipers and Wessel de Jonge build on this framework by extending the "Site" and "Access" layers to include the impact of the "Setting/Surroundings" and considering the dual nature of the "Skin" layer (both internal and external). (Kuipers and de Jonge 2017, 33–64) They also integrate the notion of the "Spirit of a Place," which encompasses the intangible, yet perceptible qualities of an area that influence its character. Although quantifying the "Spirit of a Place" in evaluation methods is challenging, the concept is vital for contextualizing and enriching results. This idea echoes the earlier concept of the "inhabitants' soul," an invisible but significant layer that Stewart Brand considers and which is rooted in Norberg-Schulz's notion of "Genius Loci." (Norberg-Schulz 1980) The sequence of impacts caused by deterioration under the shearing layers perspective in buildings had not been systematically studied until recent years. However, the last practical experiments have demonstrated their promising methodological impacts.[32]

Morphological perspectives

Flexibility and adaptability? In adaptive reuse, flexibility can be defined as the capability of space to provide distinct choices, configurations, and customizations. (Groak 2002) The border between "flexibility" and "adaptability" is blurred.[33] By this definition, a building can be adaptive but not flexible, and vice versa.[34] Flexibility often refers to addressing users' evolving physical needs, such as changes due to aging or reduced mobility. Unlike adaptation, which encompasses a broad spectrum of adjustments, flexibility specifically targets these physical changes. (Schneider and Till 2007) Despite this distinction, the literature generally views flexibility as a pathway to achieving adaptation. The studies on the flexibility of buildings are rooted in John Habraken's theory. As mentioned when referring to potential as the capability to change, John Habraken's "Supports/Infill" theory is suitable for distinguishing the construction components according to diverse building levels, such as urban tissue, supports, and infill.[35] (Habraken 1991) On this basis, Stephen Kendall developed the "Open Building" concept, (Kendall 1999) where building are divided into elements and a built environment, encompassing a multidisciplinary team of professionals and considering user participation as a crucial ingredient.[36]

What affects flexibility/adaptability in spatial terms? The most commonly used design strategies for achieving flexibility in designing new buildings could be organized into ten clusters,[37] where the physical adaptability of buildings has been classified using availability, extendibility, flexibility, refitability, movability, and recyclability as indicators. (Slaughter 2001; Schmidt et al. 2009) Dimensional and morphological features such as size, height, depth, and internal layout might decrease or increase the flexibility of buildings. (Gann and Barlow 1996, 55–66) The importance of the size and height of buildings, in terms of depth and internal layout, is a well-known condition for their capability to adapt to multiple changes in use. For instance, the more open the plan, the more the internal layout can vary. (Gann and Barlow 1996) Nevertheless, internal height and building width contribute to creating a generic space, where generality means the ability to meet changing uses or needs without changing spatial properties. (Arge 2005)

However, in the context of adaptive reuse, the concept of flexibility we refer to as spatial adaptability is intrinsically linked to the condition of the existing building. Some buildings can host more functional uses than others thanks to their original spatial flexibility, which makes them more adaptable than others in the process of adaptive reuse. Such flexibility hinges on the building's spatial redundancy—its surplus in surface area and volume—which allows for the potential expansion of uses within currently unused spaces. (Robiglio 2017, 202; Schneider and Till 2007, 181–82; Bergevoet and van Tuijl 2016) In terms of building adaptation, Douglas provides an extensive review of the possibilities of adapting historical buildings in terms of feasibility, basic conversions, and adaptive reuse. Therefore, he focuses on types of changes such as lateral extensions, vertical extensions, and structural alterations. In this case, adaptations comprehend flexibility but include additions and structural interventions. Moreover, some structural systems are better suited to changes in internal layout than others.[38] The "load-bearing redundancy" frees eventual adaptive reuse projects from structural constraints, as many industrial buildings demonstrate. (Robiglio 2017, 202) Should we therefore speak of morphological flexibility as spatial adaptability of existing building forms?

However, while focusing on morphological flexibility, up to now, the central attempts to quantitatively assess flexibility mainly follow variation and adaptations based on Habraken's theory (De Paris and Lopes 2018) and, in some cases, include Stewart Brand's "shearing layers."[39] Assessing these "adaptation potentials" in real estate has become crucial, with a focus on developing indicators to quantify a building's adaptability and providing useful evaluation criteria for decision-making, while still lacking the overall design, space, and materials of this urban legacy. This raises the question of whether focusing on a building's physical features and time-related intervention strategies might offer a more integrated approach than merely summing parameters or assessing obsolescence rates.

It is relevant to mention that all these studies focus on specific building types (i.e., houses, offices) while defining the nature of typology based on functional classification itself. Stemming from Jean-Nicolas-Louis Durand's architectural re-drawing of ancient structures at an analog scale to classify them according to formal characteristics, it is possible to outline cross-features between them. (Durand and Legrand 1801; Villari 1990) If flexibility means the capability to change to meet evolving needs, that could serve diverse functional purposes of the same building over its life. Speaking in terms of morphology, the features that emerge as drivers of flexibility are not related to functional purpose but rely on formal qualities of space (dimensions, height, weight, internal layout, space redundancy, load-bearing capacity) and management processes over time.

Form and deformations. Perhaps any object possessing inherent qualities related to its material and form is capable of being repurposed in unexpected ways, exemplifying the essence of transformative potential in morpho-structural terms. A prime example is Enzo Mari's "Ecolo," a work that provides a toolkit for transforming ordinary soap containers into unique, customized flowerpots. (Mari 1992) An object can perform a different function that requires a similar capacity to the original one: in this case, containing a liquid substance.

The Cambridge Dictionary defines the term deformation as "the action of spoiling the usual and true shape of something, or a change in its usual and true shape." (Cambridge University 2024b)

Form variation, a modification of form, requires defining what "form" means in architecture. Defining architectural form as a dual structuring of matter and space—commonly referred to by architects as the "full" and the "empty"—embraces a purely morphological, yet inclusive, perspective. (Borie et al. 1978, 24) This definition shares some similarities with Edmund Bacon's conception of the architectural form as "the point of contact between mass and space." (Bacon 1967, 16) Moreover, Bacon specifies that built forms outline the character of each culture that has produced them in terms of human attitude toward the environment. (ibid.) According to Friedman, forms from the outside can be "monomorphic" (a body without any articulation) and "polymorphic" (a composite body made of several elementary forms). Such external features of forms concern all artefacts, they are not exclusive to architecture, and they might not match an internal form: "External forms do not depend on internal forms, outside and inside are independent." (Dardi 1987, 245)

In the quest to make complex concepts more accessible, manuals often seek to clarify definitions for easy understanding and practical application. In this context, "form" is a versatile term that encompasses multiple dimensions. In these terms, "form" integrates both internal and external structures into a cohesive three-dimensional framework, encompassing the aspects of composition and configuration. (Ching 1979, 34) Relying on these definitions, any changes in the ex-ante condition of form represent a kind of deformation. Besides, these authors refer to manipulating ideal form through the design process, not the act of modifying existing built forms through an architectural project. However, they consider buildings related to their surrounding urban tissue an essential driver of deformation attitudes.

Deformation regards the manipulation of form as a configurative whole encompassing functional use. The deformation process, implied in any building, occurs by employing external solicitations coming from a context of continuous, though slow, transformation, or through architectural design interventions. (Borie et al. 1978)

According to Paul Byard, "variation depends on the potential contribution of the old to the expression of the combined work." In other words, the quality of the existing architectural form influences the deformation's success, but the final output integrates new forms through a deformation process. (Byard 2005)

Therefore, the deformation determined by any adaptive reuse project can be considered one of the phases in the evolution of the building and its reference context, to be necessarily read from a process perspective. As Stewart Brand argues, "First we shape our buildings, then they shape us, then we shape them again, ad infinitum. Function reforms form, perpetually."[40]

A change of function affects the stability of form due to its adaptive reuse or its abandonment (any function). Defining function-form relationships encompasses many authors, along with architectural theory.[41] In the field of adaptive reuse, (new) function(s) follows (existing) form. Nevertheless, the analysis of form is an established method for studying architecture and transferring notions through the redesign and schematization of buildings. (Ching 1979; Clark and Pause 1985) As Figure 9 summarizes, inquiries of form have a long tradition in architectural studies. Durand represents the first attempt at analytical analysis by exploring the building types through the lens of their formal asset. Roger Clark and Michael Pause study existing buildings by analyzing, among the other layers, their geometry, in plan and section, to retrace shape proportions and composition.

Francis D.K. Ching divides the configuration of buildings in several ways, mainly: central; linear; radial; clustered; and grid. (Ching 1979) In doing so, he remarks that transformations of forms can be understood to be "transformations of the primary solids or variations of its dimensions," (Ching 1979, 34) where "transformation" is one of the principles of form. In this case, transformation is explored from the perspective of prior experiences. (ibid.) In addition, Alain Borie, Pierre Micheloni, and Pierre Pinon analyze deformation types by defining volume, envelope, partition, interior spaces, and interior envelope. (Borie et al. 1978) These authors analyze design as a generative process based on obtaining a series of "finite permutations" to be used in designing new buildings. Therefore, considering the field of design on existing buildings, adaptive reuse is an action that might modify its form in terms of the structure of the space, mass, internal or external outline, three-dimensional composition and configuration.

Introducing the term configuration over the term composition leads to joining functional and formal qualities of architecture. The idea that separating form from content might lead to a misleading division that prompts us to embrace a broader concept of configuration. This approach connects both functional and formal aspects, providing a more integrated understanding. (Kurrent 1978, 6–10) In the reuse intervention for an abandoned building, only through a project might it be possible to assess the compatible level of hybridization by placing the new intervention on the only historically and culturally legitimate ground, that of the search for relationships between ancient and modern in terms of congruency between measure and figure. (Dardi 1987, 245)

Interventions and actions. Despite the diffusion of morphological studies and intervention analysis, the integration between morphology and adaptive reuse approaches in adaptive reuse literature seems still under-explored, (Fisher-Gewirtzman 2016) especially independently from the functional types. Regarding the intervention types in adaptive reuse, the so-called form-form approach to adaptive reuse analyzes the relationship between the preexistence in its formal qualities and the following intervention strategies. (Plevoets and Van Cleempoel 2019) This approach focuses mainly on the form-form relationships. Adaptive interventions are addressed in terms of a formal relationship with the existing building. As pointed out by Bie Plevoets and Koenraad Van Cleempoel (2019), these classifications of intervention types in adaptive reuse follow Rodolfo Machado's strategic approach. (Machado 1976) Several authors are included in the form-form approach. In particular, Philippe Robert (1989) identifies 7 approaches,[42] Edward T. White (1999) introduces more than 20 types of adaptive intervention,[43] and Graeme Brooker and Sally Stone focus on the modification of the existing buildings, defining three main strategies for adaptation—"installation," "insertion," and "intervention." Frank P. Jäger follows a similar approach, outlining classifying examples—"transformation," "addition," and "conversion." (Jäger 2012) Françoise A. Bollack categorizes case studies into five types based on how the adaptation interacts with the existing structure.[44] (Bollack 2013) Liliane Wong, on the other hand, describes existing buildings as "host structures"—"entity," "shell," "semi-ruin," "fragmented," "relic," and "group"—and frames intervention in three types of actions—"passive," "performative," and "referential,"—while the adaptive reuse processes are listed in terms of "mathematics operations" to clarify the relationship between the host's form and the interventions. (Wong 2016) Expanding on these approaches, the potential of the form should transcend the simple dichotomy between host and intervention. It should encompass the dimensions of time and completeness, as well as address how the form itself—as a stage of space and matter—deforms and evolves throughout the adaptive reuse process.

Energy dynamics of form

Tectonics vs. functions. Across morphology and materials, what if we embrace a post-functional approach? The potential for a building to change can be understood through a framework similar to that of an ecosystem, where a hierarchy of components influences the dynamics of the system. In such systems, slower elements often dominate the dynamics, while faster elements follow behind. (O'Neill et al. 2021) Similarly, a building can be analyzed by breaking it down into its components, which can be assessed based on specific criteria.[45] Concepts like "stereotomy" and "tectonics" further refine this classification by focusing on the building's essential elements.[46]

Stereotomy deals with heavy building elements, dividing a structure into components like earthwork, hearth, framework, roof, and enclosing membranes. Tectonics, on the other hand, focuses on light and linear elements within a building.[47] Structure and materials function together to achieve a "building's tectonic value."[48] By embedding a building within a framework that highlights its tectonic features—focusing on its spatial and material aspects—, we establish a foundation for extending this approach to other buildings regardless of their original function. Tectonic systems, which integrate both spatial and material dynamics, offer a streamlined classification in "morpho-structural" types. However, such tectonic types are not mutually exclusive and represent a simplification of reality. Real buildings present hybrid systems that often combine diverse tectonic types assembled in a unique structure.

A theoretical reference to a typological shift from a functional to such a morphological classification is here embedded in the idea of the *Idealtypus*, posited in Max Weber's "The Methodology of the Social Sciences." Weber introduced the *Idealtypus* as a specific method of concept formation in social sciences. (Hadorn

1997) This ideal type represents a conceptual framework that is not historical reality nor the "true or genuine" reality, though it more or less serves as a scheme by which reality must be subsumed as a template; it signifies a pure and limited boundary notion, whereby reality must be measured and compared to illustrate the significant determining elements of its empiric essence. (Weber et al. 1949) Such a methodological framework is not present in the real world; however, it shares some features with real objects, even if it does not derive from them. This concept implicates a phenomenological approach to reality, rooted in the concept of potential itself. (Reiser and Umemoto 2006; Goethe et al. 1863) However, several studies expound the process of assembling construction materials not just by classifying buildings according to their essential materials, neither by their structure or the tectonic type in general, but also by considering the building itself as a storage of "already consumed" energy.[49]

Materials and energy. The energy embedded in the building's materials and construction process is termed "embodied energy."[50] It is important to note that embodied energy might be a key to analyzing materials and built structures only when inserted within the framework of a multidisciplinary approach, asserting the fluid nature of architectural studies. The appeal of embodied energy was accentuated from an architectural standpoint owing to the current efforts toward expanding the boundaries of this field. (Benjamin 2017) The narrative of adaptive reuse highlights the concept that existing buildings embody such a latent value in the form of energy itself, which, when recognized and harnessed, can positively influence cultural, economic, and social development. (Douglas, 2006; Robiglio, 2017; Oswalt, 2008) In the 1970s, embodied energy was defined for existing structures as the amount of energy required to process and arrange building materials in place, and this energy is not recoverable. (ACHP 1979)

On the other hand, a relatively recent definition defines embodied energy as the energy existing in building materials and the energy necessary to produce and maintain buildings, which introduces a lifecycle perspective. (Monteiro 2015) This embodied energy can be described as "retroactive embodied energy," encompassing the energy expenditures incurred in the past that are non-recoverable and pertain to existing structures before any new intervention, whether demolition, new construction, or adaptation. (Guidetti and Ferrara 2023) These assumptions might be applied to existing buildings by recognizing that a considerable energy investment has been made in constructing the built environment. Therefore, the demolition of existing buildings implies a waste of costly energy resources already in place. The transformation of existing buildings entails the removal or recovery of existing materials and the addition of new construction materials. Indeed, valuing the avoidance of demolition and waste of energy is in itself a critical principle, since "the greenest building is the one already built." (Elefante, 2012) A key aspect of this "untapped potential" is embodied energy, which refers to the energy consumed in the construction of a building that remains locked within its fabric. This concept has gained increasing attention in redevelopment projects, leading to a deeper exploration and interpretation of its implications. (Guidetti and Ferrara 2023;

Mourão et al. 2019; Birgisdottir et al. 2017; Gaspar and Santos 2015; Monteiro 2015; Jackson 2005; ACHP 1979)

To bridge the gap between theory and practice, pilot calculations on representative case studies are essential to address retroactive embodied energy in real cases. While structural systems and materials define spatial assets and energy assemblages, they are mutually influenced by the passage of time and multiple other external factors in a dynamic and complex system of transformations. (Cairns and Jacobs 2014, 220–32) Retroactive embodied energy is a powerful argument and an avoidable component of the transformative potential.

Assessing retroactive embodied energy. The concept of retroactive embodied energy serves as a proxy to analyze materials in adapted buildings and their impact across the evolution of form. This method will evaluate this energy in two main stages: the existing building and the adaptive reuse intervention. In the latter stage, deconstructive and constructive actions will be equally taken into account. The survey model is based on the assumption that most of the embodied energy in a building is contained in the bulk of the architectural materials.[51] This calculation employs the survey method outlined in the Advisory Council on Historical Preservation's 1979 report, "Assessing the Energy Conservation Benefits of Historic Preservation: Method and Examples." (ACHP 1979) The original formula evaluates embodied energy by summing the Embodied Energy in Construction (EIC) and the Energy Invested in Materials (EIM). The approach applied here focuses on the EIC to highlight the impact of materials added during adaptive reuse, using a simplified version of the survey method.

EIM = 1.4 * Σ [Quantity of material * Invested Energy per Material Unit (IEM)]
(The factor 1.4 is an adjustment coefficient to account for the fact that the survey model covers only about 50% of the total embodied energy in building construction, according to ACHP)

This formula approximates the embodied energy involved before and after the adaptive reuse process within a cradle-to-gate boundary system. The evaluation of embodied energy for construction materials uses ICE database version 2.0, (Hammond and Jones 2011) developed by the University of Bath and based on European data, where embodied impact is expressed in MJ/kg.[52] IEM values are then converted to MJ/sqm to correspond with the 3D model unit measure for each building.

The transformative potential of form is a mutual relationship between relative variations of space and matter in a specific time and located in a specific context.

Where:
Space is a sum of dimensional and morphological features.

Matter includes the primary materials structuring the space and their relative (retroactive) embodied energy.

Time is the span between "as found" and "as transformed."

The context is post-functional Europe.

CROSS-LENSES IN POST-FUNCTIONAL FRAMEWORKS: SETTING THE RULES

How to address this transformative potential of form? The following section refines the concept of transformative potential by focusing on the mutual relationships between spatial and material variations in a specific temporal and geographical context to integrate these factors into a cohesive understanding of the transformative process. How do space and matter interact over time in adaptive reuse approaches? This analysis seeks to display and highlight patterns that reveal the transformative potential of architectural form, ultimately contributing to more nuanced and effective approaches in adaptive reuse.

A phenomenological approach to the case studies

The following book section summarizes a multiple case study analysis focusing on 16 building adaptations. Cases were selected for their physical qualities within a "post-functional" framework, meaning they were considered purely for their variety in terms of formal features. The analysis adopts a phenomenological approach, beginning with an in-depth examination of each case, critical redrawing, a 3D model of each case, and morphological schemes. Alongside these main cases, the study briefly includes additional examples and unexpected cases identified during the extensive 40-day fieldwork.[53]

The selected 16 cases represent various morpho-structural types and levels of decay, showcasing a spectrum of interventions from minimal to extensive. The analysis uses three methods—decay stages in shearing layers, morphological analysis, and embodied energy evaluation—to explore transformations from multiple perspectives of these case studies divided into four groups based on their relative completeness.

The concept of *Idealtypus* is employed to adopt a phenomenological approach to the case studies,[54] starting from the selection phase and influencing the entire research. Here, elements making up a complex system, such as a plant (or a building), might be investigated starting from their capabilities to evolve.[55]

Historically, typologies are predictive categories to be applied to reality; here, the intent is to address a novel classification of buildings. The goal is to underline the transformative potential as the evolution of form in terms of decay, space, and matter. To do so, the criteria set to determine this classification of ideal types assume the following morpho-structural types as a template of reality for case study selection.

Three key criteria are used to isolate these morpho-structural types: the tectonics of structural elements (Hurol 2015) and the basic dimensions of height and size. The tectonics of structure comprehends structural assets and materials, relying on the assumption that structural systems represent the exoskeleton of the building form, and each possible match between these parameters represents a possible morpho-structural type. The case study selection embraces the possibilities of "incomplete" buildings for analysis, enlarging the definition of the building itself.[56] Thus,

Morpho-structural types

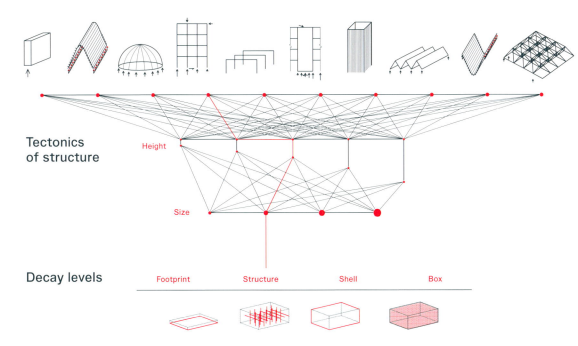

Scheme of case study organization by morpho-structural types in terms of completeness

none of the selected preexisting buildings has not yet undergone any decay process. All the cases were "dismissed" buildings, abandoned, and not hosting any function; in other words, all the cases presented were in "absolute obsolescence" before the adaptive reuse intervention. This obsolescence is "the condition referring to the state of the building itself, regardless of the state of other buildings or user demands." This obsolescence encompasses an obvious functional decay.[57] (Abramson 2016; Buitelaar et al. 2021)

Post-functional Europe

The post-functional framework serves as a boundary system for this analysis, providing a post-structuralist perspective to investigate buildings based on their physical form and transformative potential. The term "post-functional Europe" refers to both the geographic and cultural contexts of the analysis and the nature of the buildings examined. Here, "post-functional" denotes buildings that no longer serve their original purposes and are not defined by stable functions. This condition is particularly evident in dismissed buildings, adapted for new uses and seen as vessels of memory with inherent value beyond their original functions. The analysis centers on the buildings' forms, independent of legal, normative, and functional concerns. The "post-functional" framework highlights buildings that have either lost their original function or been repurposed, focusing on how their forms can persist and be adapted across different functional changes. This approach reflects the modern emphasis on functional flexibility, a concept that has gained prominence since the 1980s. Yona Friedman's intuition seems to find a place in contemporary architectural trends (Friedman et al. 2015) as evidenced by the "Supports/Infill" theory and in the "Open Building" approach. (Habraken 1991; Kendall 1999) The post-functional framework focuses on spatial relationships among functionally heterogeneous buildings, following the intuition that diverse typologies of buildings, like a Gothic cathedral and the Crystal Palace, might share similar spatial and structural characteristics that affect their adaptation.[58] Moreover, as buildings adapt to new purposes over time, their original functional elements become less relevant, shifting the focus to their form.

The 16 case studies selected are organized into four main groups based on a completeness average: 1) Footprints, 2) Structures, 3) Shells, and 4) Boxes. The category "Footprints" includes fragments of buildings, such as foundations, a single wall, or a few traces in the ground. The group labeled "Structures" comprises cases where only the structure resisted the passage of time, with no shell; in other words, only the pillars and beams have survived. "Shells" are buildings that partially define an "interior" and an "exterior" space; in other words, pillars and beams with a roof and (partial) envelope. The last group, "Boxes," refers to complete buildings in terms of structure, with shell and interior organization. This group includes well-conserved architectures, even if systems, façades, and interior layout are outdated.[59]

A definition of each category in terms of potential will be proposed at the end of the analysis.

The triplets' interplay

As mentioned previously, these three primary methods are used to develop an integrated approach for capturing the transformative potential by maximizing the complex interplay of the form transformation of buildings over time: 1) evaluation of decay stages; 2) morphological analysis; and 3) embodied energy assessment.

1) The evaluation of decay stages explores constructive and deconstructive actions using the Shearing Layers Theory. Grounded in intervention theory, this analysis assesses building development over time by examining the evolution of various layers—such as site, structure, and skin—before and after adaptive reuse interventions. Each case study is analyzed in terms of layer completeness and the fixity of these layers, focusing primarily on the most permanent elements, like the structure. Constructive actions refer to adaptive interventions that add, replace, or complete layers, while deconstructive actions involve the removal or demolition of layers. This framework highlights the ongoing transformation of buildings over time.
2) The morphological analysis method critically examines form and deformation in adaptive reuse projects. It assesses changes in dimensional features—such as plan, height, and volume—before and after interventions, using drawings, reports, and data. Critical redrawing and 3D models help visualize how buildings evolve within their urban context, emphasizing changes in massing and spatial organization.[60]

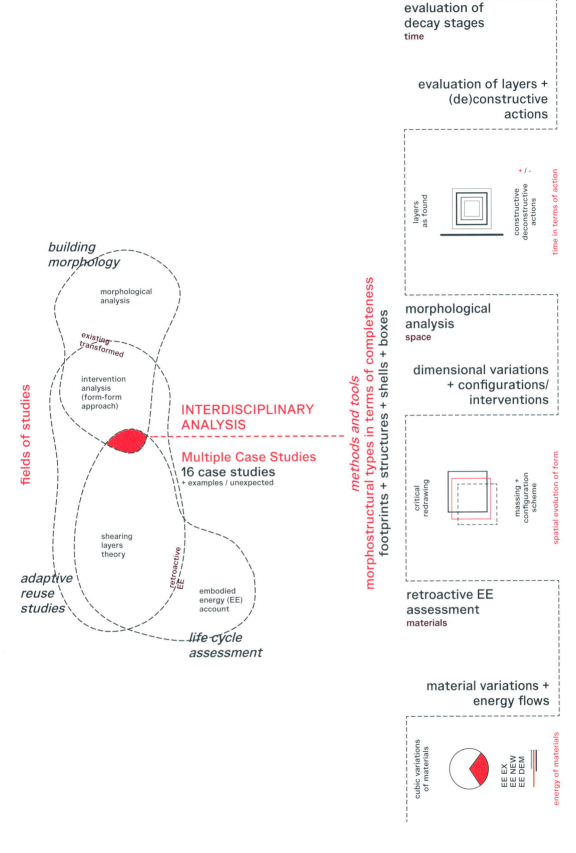

Cross-lenses in post-functional frameworks: setting the rules 57

Configurative schemes further analyze the structural and spatial systems, revealing how adaptive reuse reshapes buildings while maintaining a relationship with their original form and surroundings.

3) The embodied energy and materials assessment method examines the energy required to produce, transform, and assemble materials in adaptive reuse projects. This analysis focuses on structural materials, assumed to be resistant to decay, and evaluates how material use impacts form transformation and sustainability. The assessment compares embodied energy in two stages: the original building and the adaptive reuse intervention, accounting for both constructive and deconstructive actions. Using a simplified survey method, embodied energy is calculated based on the bulk materials, primarily structural elements, and the building envelope, which typically contain the highest levels of embodied energy.[61]

This methodological integration aims to merge the dynamics of time, space, and materials in examining the potential transformation of existing buildings.[62]

Endnotes

1   The Etymonline repository collects the main sources across etymological dictionaries. Available at https://www.etymonline.com/columns/post/sources?utm_source=etymonline_footer&utm_medium=link_exchange. Accessed on 06/08/2024. In particular, see (Etymonline 2024).

2   Potentiel, elle might be an adjective with similar meaning to the English version; as a noun, it refers to the following: 1. *gramm. mode potentiel*, 2. *technique-scientifique*: p. *mécanique, électrique, statique*, etc., (*terme médical*). XIV sec. Empr.du lat. Potential*is* (*de potentia*, v. *potence*); *étendu ensuite à d'autres techn.*

3   Plato discerns the purchasing power and the persuasion power in the Laws, book 11, section 918b. (918b) In the work *Republic*, Plato stated that each art is different from the others because its power itself is different; they differ in terms of potentials as diverse kind of powers. (Muscato 2005)

4   The philosopher Giorgio Agamben defines the "paradigm of operativity" as "a process that was present as from the very beginning of Western ontology, [...] a tendency to resolve, or at least to indeterminate, being into acting" where *dynamis* and *energeia* are "two ways in which being is said," implicitly arguing that it contains an "orientation of being toward operativity." (Agamben 2013, 57)

5   Carl Friedrich Gauss re-presented the first publication on *the potential* theory by George Green. In 1828, Green published his studies on the *potential* function, but he was not involved enough in academia to receive credits for it. Thanks to Gauss, the use of the term "potential" as the short form for the "potential function" became popular. (Gauss 2009; Green 1828)

6   In this fresco, Aristotle points the finger to the earth (as the realm of things), while Plato indicates the sky (the realm of forms). School of Athens, fresco by Raphael, 1508–11, in the *Stanza della Segnatura*, the Vatican.

7   In Aristotelian metaphysics, the active, determining principle of a thing is distinguished from matter, the potential principle. Matter is the potential factor, form the actualizing factor. (Duignan 2019)

8   For a more comprehensive understanding of this concept, refer to Aristotle, *Metaphysics*, Θ.1, 1046a12; Z 1048b1–3.

9   Manuel Delanda interprets Gilles Deleuze (1988, 97) who describes the real as metric space and linear time, and the virtual as immanent. According to this reading, certain situations reveal the "morphogenetic potential of matter" through an "objective illusion," while others do not. This illusion might provide a "window to the virtual," which is otherwise observable only by nudging a material system from equilibrium to an "intensive" non-equilibrium. (DeLanda et al. 2005, 76)

10	In quantum field theory and quantum mechanics, the term "propagator" specifies the probability amplitude for a particle to move from one place to another in a given timeframe.
11	For instance, realizing the ability to be a doctor (to heal) is also realizing the ability to be a poisoner. (Scheffler 1985, vol. 25, chap. 2)
12	*A cabinet of curiosities*.
13	Price and Littlewood found a site for building the Fun Palace in East London, on the banks of the Lea River. However, bureaucrats in the local planning office halted the project, and the Fun Palace was never completed. (Stanley 2006)
14	See Coop Himmelb(l)au's works: the Musée de Confluence, Lyon, France (2014) and the Falkestrasse Rooftop Remodeling, Vienna, Austria (1988).
15	In Vitruvius's work, the triad of qualities comprises *utilitas* (refers to function, commodity, and utility), *firmitas* (refers to solidity and materiality), and *venustas* (relates to beauty, delight, and desire). The last one, since it deals with aesthetics, has not been considered functional to the current discourse, as it would require a wide specific explanation.
16	See the definition of "*Genius loci*" in Encyclopedia Britannica where "Genius" (Latin: *begetter*; plural *Genii*) is defined as "in classical Roman times, an attendant spirit of a person or place." Available at https://www.britannica.com/topic/genius-Roman-religion. Accessed on 08/08/2024.
17	Projects like Sigurd Lewerentz and Gunnar Asplund's Woodland Cemetery demonstrate how architectural intervention can reveal a site's inherent potential, in this case, recognizing the forest as an integral part of the design. Similarly, Frank Lloyd Wright's Fallingwater harnesses the natural forces of its site, transforming the landscape's constraints into a generative design element. These examples illustrate how architecture can make visible the hidden possibilities of a place.
18	Consider the concept of situation or configuration (形 *xing*) that was previously analyzed.
19	In the first chapter, "Transformation and control," N.J. Habraken defined "change" as one of the four pillars of his research. (Habraken 2000, 6–7) The relation between potential and flexibility is discussed in the next subchapter.
20	These buildings are designed for adaptation to allow for future expansion of medical services as technology advances. To accomplish this, the concept is organized as a roadway system with buildings that may be used and extended as needed.
21	See "Potential as indeterminate."
22	Goethe wrote in a letter to German poet Johann Gottfried Herder, "one will be able to invent plants without limit to conform, that is to say, plants which even if they do not actually exist nevertheless might exist." (von Goethe 1952, 14) Then he added, "What effect does a general element in its various modifications have upon one and the same form?" (ibid., 47)
23	See the concept of potential as "latent" and "indeterminate" and as a "loss."
24	As Matteo Robiglio pointed out: To activate this dormant potential, it is crucial to consider the location (accessibility, connection, services, neighboring areas, visibility, and view). In addition, it is fundamental to define the appropriate scale of intervention—in particular, "context and goals define the right scale and form of projects." The next important aspect is to focus on how the potential of the existing area shall be maximized. (Robiglio 2017, 150–53)
25	See "potential as loss."
26	See the exhibition report "Cronocaos." Available at https://www.oma.com/projects/venice-biennale-2010-cronocaos. Accessed on 09/08/2024.
27	See "Architectures Transformées / Transformative architectures" at the Arsenale Pavilion in Venice, October 1997- January 1998. Curated by Philippe Simon and Edith Girard. Available at https://www.pavillon-arsenal.com/en/expositions/9610-transformative-architecture.html. Accessed on 08/09/2024.
28	See Table 2.7 in (Douglas 2006, 71).
29	To support his discourse, Daniel Abramson cites the "Functional Obsolescence" graph by Peter Cowan. (University of London, 1963)
30	Deterioration and decay might outline a direct relationship between age and increasing value, stemming from Riegl's "Theory of Values." (Riegl 1984) According to Alois Riegl, age value (*Alterswert*) is independent of other qualities (particularly material, technical execution, destination, historical, and aesthetic significance). On the other hand, this conception might cause that every building enjoys the right of protection only because it has existed for a certain period of time.
31	In 1999, Stewart Brand also introduced the concept of "pace layers" that refers to the idea that within a complex system—such as society, an ecosystem, or a business context—different layers evolve at varying speeds, ranging from rapid to slow. (Brand 2000)
32	An example of practical applications in sustainable (de)construction, renovation, and reuse is the study conducted by ROTOR. Since January 2019, ROTOR has been leading an Interreg NWE project titled FCRBE (Facilitating the Circulation of Reclaimed Building Elements in Northwestern Europe). This project applies the Shearing Layers Theory to building components to ease their reuse potential. For detailed insights, refer to the research report "Ex-post Analysis of 32 Construction and Renovation

33 There is disagreement on the significance of the terms flexibility and adaptability regarding the rate of change, frequency, and magnitude. (Askar et al. 2021) For instance, some authors consider flexibility changes as being short-term, speedier, and of a lesser magnitude, whereas adaptation indicates larger-scale, major-scale changes over long periods of time. (Leaman et al. 1998)

34 The studies on flexibility started during the 1970s, especially in the context of housing systems, where "flexibility" is advocated as an alternative to "tight-fit functionalism," meant as the scenario of mass housing in Europe during the twentieth century. (De Paris and Lopes 2018; Rabeneck and Sheppard 1973)
According to Herman Hertzberger, "flexibility" suggests an open-ended solution, (Hertzberger et al. 2005) also called the "rhetoric value" of flexibility by Tatiana Schneider and Jeremy Till. (Schneider and Till 2007) They refer to the term flexibility as proposing different solutions for diverse users, shifting the target from a single solution to the most appropriate solution according to specific needs, following the attitude "of continually asking of the ability of that piece of design and construction to be adapted over time;" in addition, "generic principles" provide maximum flexibility. (ibid.)

35 In particular, the system improved by the Foundation for Architectural Research (SAR) is considered a key strategy of flexibility. Stephen Kendall describes SAR (Stichting Architecten Research or Foundation for Architects' Research) as follow: "SAR was founded in the Netherlands in 1965 to stimulate industrialization in housing. More generally, it sought to study issues surrounding the relationship between the architecture profession and the housing industry, and to chart new directions for architects in housing design." Available at http://www.open-building.org/gloss/sar.html. Accessed on 11/11/2023

36 Open Building was launched in the Netherlands as a not-for-profit "Open Building Society" in the eighties to pursue the implementation of the "Supports/Infill" approach as earlier advocated by SAR. This society was active until 2000, when it was decided that its goals were now sufficiently accepted by the government and industry. The task group TG26 was instituted in 1996 by Seiji Sawada from Japan, Stephen Kendall from the USA, and Karel Dekker from the Netherlands. In 2000, the task group became the permanent Work Group W104, guided by Stephen Kendall (USA), Kazunobu Minami (Japan), and Beishi Jia (Hong Kong). Available online at https://www.habraken.com/html/introduction.htm. Accessed on 09/09/2021.

37 Reduce intersystem interactions, dedicate specific area/volume for system zone, reduce intra-system interactions, enhance system access proximity, use interchangeable system components, improve flow, increase layout predictability, phase system installation, improve physical access, simplify partial/phased demolition

38 James Douglas emphasizes that feasibility can be assessed through three main categories: viability (economic feasibility), practicality (physical feasibility), and utility (functional feasibility). He highlights that frame systems are generally more adaptable than masonry construction systems. (Douglas 2006)

39 The main methods in real estate studies are: 1) the Adaptive Capacity (AC) method that evaluates the sustainable impact of reusing versus constructing new buildings. According to Wilkinson, adaptability and sustainability are closely linked. The AC approach helps building owners and users assess whether to buy, build new, or remodel an existing structure. It involves considering the perspectives of owners, users, and society, with a focus on long-term profitability, adaptability to changing needs, and attractiveness for future users. The method is divided into two phases: user dynamics, which address individual needs, and transformation dynamics, which focus on the building level. (Geraedts et al. 2014; Wilkinson and Remøy 2011) Flexibility studies within AC, rooted in theories by John N. Habraken and Tatiana Schneider and Jeremy Till, explore various levels such as destination, urban tissue, and construction. Factors influencing flexibility include demountable components, service locations, and adaptable features like façades and floor heights. (Habraken 1991; Schneider and Till 2007); 2) The FLEX methods that assesses the adaptive reuse capacity of buildings through a series of indicators. The initial FLEX 1.0 version used 147 indicators divided into user and owner levels but was later simplified. FLEX 2.0 introduced Brand's five shearing layers, with 83 indicators and a weighted scoring system. FLEX 2.0 Light further streamlined the method to 17 indicators for a quicker assessment. FLEX 3.0 focused on specific building types, such as schools and offices, using 44 indicators across various building layers. The latest FLEX 4.0 version separates indicators into two categories: 12 general indicators and 32 specific ones for schools and offices. (Geraedts 2016; Geraedts and Prins 2015) While previous versions were useful for various scales, FLEX 4.0 offers detailed and broad evaluations based on building type; 3) The Adaptive Reuse Potential (ARP) model evaluates buildings based on their useful life, considering physical, economic, functional, technological, social, legal, and political obsolescence. This model, which uses a discount rate

	to determine a building's reuse potential, provides a percentage score for adaptive reuse potential. The ARP model helps prioritize existing buildings for reuse and can be updated with strategic investments to extend a building's useful life. (Langston 2012; Langston et al. 2013) For a literature review on the topic see (Amiri 2019).
40	Stewart Brand integrates Louis Sullivan and Winston Churchill's divergent thoughts about the form-function relationship in buildings, while introducing the dynamic of time. (Brand 1995, 3)
41	Louis Sullivan created the expression "Form Follows Function" in his article "The Tall Office Building Artistically Considered" in 1896. (Sullivan 1896) The adage "Form always follows function" was founded on Vitruvius's Roman concepts of architecture being sturdy, functional, and attractive. (Pollio et al., 1914). Based on this conception, in the design phase, functions of the spaces take precedence but include other elements. The program or function of the space affected and resulted in the tectonics, materials, textures, shapes, and colors. For instance, Adrian Forty examines the term function since the 1930s, remarks on its confusing interpretations, and analyzes the historical evolution of the word "function," as well as how it has influenced architectural forms and discourse throughout history. One of his interpretations of "form" integrates the German terms *sachlich*, *zweckmässig*, and *funktionell*, reflecting a comprehensive understanding of functionality. In particular, function as "*zweckmässig*," means "purpose," which encompasses both the fulfillment of material requirements (utility) and biological purpose (destiny). This consideration might outline the function as a connotation of form without establishing a predominance of function over form. Moreover, Yona Friedman proposes the statement "function follows form," following a dynamic process of architecture articulated in three steps with a growing degree of fixity: function maps (topological graphs), buildings' envelopes, and supporting structures. (Friedman 2000, 110) Brand remarks "form follows funding," underlining the building as a propriety at first that is driven by commerce as all proprieties are. (Brand 1995, 5) To deepen the form-function relationship in Modernism and in contemporary theories see (Poerschke 2016).
42	—"building within," "building over," "building around," "building alongside," "recycling materials or vestiges," "adapting to a new function," and "building in the style of" (Robert 1989)
43	—"corner," "wall," "gate," "hat," "parasite," "roof," "underground," "joint," "transition," "bridge," "skin," "new interior," "divider," "umbrella," "filter," "infill," etc. (White 1999)
44	—"insertions," "parasites," "wraps," "juxtapositions," and "weavings" (Bollack 2013)
45	For instance, building elements can be categorized by their deterioration rates (Brand 1995; Duffy 1992) or their degree of "fixity." (N. Habraken 1991; Kendall 1999)
46	As Sou Fujimoto highlights, architecture can be viewed through two archetypes: the "nest" and the "cave." (Fujimoto 2008) A "cave" represents a naturally occurring, pre-existing space that exists independently of human intervention. When a person chooses to inhabit a cave, they must adapt to its existing conditions and deal with its inherent ambiguities. In contrast, a "nest" is a human or animal creation, designed specifically for its inhabitants. It is constructed to be more prescriptive and functional, as it would not exist without human effort.
47	Gottfried Semper referred to the Vitruvius's classical triad—*utilitas* (utility), *firmitas* (stability), and *venustas* (beauty)—to differentiate between light/stable tectonics and heavy/stable stereotomy. (Semper 1851). According to Semper, the essence of tectonics lies in using diverse materials to make a cultural statement. Frampton echoed this sentiment, emphasizing that a building's form and structure significantly influence its tectonic expression. (Frampton 1995)
48	In defining structural types, Tung-Yen Lin and Sidney D. Stotesbury organized structural systems into "horizontal subsystems," "vertical subsystems," "high-rise buildings," "arch," "suspension," "shell systems," and "foundation subsystems." (Lin and Stotesbury 1988) Heino Engel identified "vector active" (such as trusses), "surface-active" (such as folded plates), "section active" (such as beams), and "form active" (such as cables). (Engel 1981) Furthermore, Jeffrey W. Place classified structures into axial members, beams, trusses, compression structures, and tensile spanning structures. (Place 2007) Finally, Yonca Hurol summarized structural systems by grouping categories of tectonics types into four families, "compression structures," "truss structures," "bending structures," and "tensile structures." (Hurol 2015) Structural systems might be classified "according to their form and the stress type they generate," and this form-stress type relationship represents a "bridge between architecture and structural engineering." (ibid., 2–6)
49	For an extensive literature review of the retroactive embodied energy see (Guidetti and Ferrara, 2023). Key references about the integration of embodied energy in architecture and adaptive reuse strategy see (Benjamin 2017; Fabian et al. 2012; Jackson 2005)
50	The concept of embodied energy was first proposed by Wassily Leontief in his article "Input-Output Economics," (Christ 1968) then diffused as a concept in *Jobs for tomorrow: the potential for substituting manpower for*

energy, (Stahel and Reday-Mulvey 1981) and transferred to the field of architecture by the National Trust publication *New Energy from Old Buildings* (Maddex and States 1981) and by the Advisory Council on Historical Preservation in *Assessing the energy conservation benefits of historic preservation: method and examples.* (ACHP 1979)

51   The Survey Model, a streamlined version of the Input-Output Method, simplifies the assessment by focusing on structural elements, the building envelope, and Energy Investment in Materials (EIM). This model is used because the structural system is the most permanent part of a building and is likely to be preserved during adaptive reuse, while the structural system and the envelope together account for up to half of the building's initial embodied energy. The embodied energy assessment aims to include environmental impacts in the reuse of buildings, emphasizing sustainability in adaptive reuse projects.

52   The updated version of the ICE database (2011) shifts the focus from embodied energy to embodied carbon. Here, however, the account follows embodied energy while leaving the option for future research to convert it into embodied carbon. (Hammond and Jones 2011)

53   The fieldwork is documented on the website "Atlas of Potential. A Grand Tour of Europe in transformation." Available at https://www.atlasofpotential.com/. In particular, see the online geo-referred and ongoing digital database "Atlas of Potential." Available at https://maps.mapifator.com/places/FGNNhKFJhsyvsW6Nt5xE.

54   The research relies on inductive reasoning and adopts a phenomenological approach to the case studies. In this approach, the elements making up a complex system are investigated considering their capabilities to evolve as the starting point, as opposed to the deductive reasoning approach that categorizes them a priori. (Reiser and Umemoto 2006, 63) Moreover, the following section embraces the assumption that an "interplay of case study research designs and theoretical contributions on the theory continuum is a prerequisite for the contribution of case study research to better theories." (Ridder 2017, 302) The approach to the case studies is itself an attempt to propose a novel methodology for the enquiry into the transformation of existing buildings.

Such an approach aspires to explore the built environment in its physical appearances—qualities that, according to the literature surrounding the concept of potential and its role in the discourse of adaptive reuse process, can have a stronger impact on the transformation of buildings when embracing a morphological perspective. It assumes goal-oriented ideal types that represent a conceptual framework, serving as a scheme by which reality must be subsumed as a template.

55   This phenomenological approach can be better understood by examining Goethe's concept of the "archetypal plant" through the lens of the concept of potential. (von Goethe 1790)

56   See the term "building" in Glossary.

57   The dynamics driving this change are multifaceted, complex, and influenced by a variety of factors beyond mere formal qualities. Here, the focus is solely on the morphological aspects of the narrative.

58   In 1961, Konrad Wachsmann suggested a spatial link between technological standardization and historical, fixed typologies, like Gothic churches, highlighting potential parallels in structural and spatial characteristics across different architectural eras. (Wachsmann 1961)

59   This grouping relies on the theory of building shearing layers adapted by Stewart Brand. (Brand 1995, 14)

60   In this regard, color code is employed, with red for the new and black for the existing. This approach has been largely employed in adaptive reuse, and it relies on the BYR (black, yellow, red) color code. (Boesch et al. 2019)

61   The method is extensively explained in the paragraph "Assessing retroactive embodied energy."

62   These analytical methods were refined and adjusted throughout an intensive 40-day fieldwork period. Spreadsheet software was used to organize and process the numerical data, while vector drawing software was used for critical redrawing and creating three-dimensional models for each case study. The author produced all graphs, drawings, and diagrams presented in this thesis.

AR POST-FUNCTIONAL FORMS:

ADAPTIVE REUSE PROJECTS THROUGH STAGES OF COMPLETENESS

In growing and changing through time, the built environment resembles an organism more than an artefact. Yet, while ever-changing, it does possess qualities that transcend time. [...] Building environment is indeed organic: continuous renewal and replacement of individual cells preserve it, giving the ability to persist. (Habraken 2000, 6–7)

Completeness	Case Study	City	AR Designer	Original use	New use	Time original/new
Footprints	Duperré Playground	Paris, FR	ILL-Studio	Parking lot	Basketball field	1850s/2012–2015–2017–2020–2024
Footprints	Can Tacó	Barcelona, SP	Toni Gironès Saderra	Roman house + administrative office	Viewpoint	2nd cen. BC/2012
Footprints	Cau Sau	Olot, SP	Un Parell d'Arquitectes	House	Stage	1900s/2019
Footprints	Basilica di Siponto	Foggia, IT	Edoardo Tresoldi	Church	Installation + event venue	1117/2016
Structures	Kraanspoor	Amsterdam, NL	OTH Architecten	Craneway	Offices	1952/2007
Structures	King's Cross Gasholders	London, UK	WilkinsonEyre	Gasometers	Residential + offices	1867/2019
Structures	Vitali Sheds	Turin, IT	Latz + Partner	Steel factory	Skatepark + event venue	1973/2011
Structures	Panorâmico de Monsanto	Lisbon, PT	Technical office of the Camera Municipal de Lisboa	Restaurant	Viewpoint + stage	1967/2017
Shells	Alvéoles	Saint-Nazaire, FR	Manuel de Sola Moralès + Gilles Clément + Coloco + LIN Architects + 51N4E + Bourbouze et Graindorge	Submarine base	Cultural center + square	1942/2002–2018
Shells	PC Caritas	Melle, BE	Architecten De Vylder Vinck Taillieu	Psychiatric pavilion	Healthcare + square	1907/2009
Shells	Cité de la Mode et du Design	Paris, FR	Jakob & MacFairlane	General stores	Cultural center	1841/2014
Shells	Szimpla Kert	Budapest, UH	N/A	Stove factory + house	Ruin pub	1908/2016
Boxes	Bourse du Commerce	Paris, FR	Tadao Ando + NeM Architects + Pierre-Antoine Gatier	Grain market	Art museum	1889/2021
Boxes	Bookstore Dominicanen	Maastricht, NL	Merkx + Girod Architecten + SATIJNplus Architecten	Church	Bookshop	1294/2007
Boxes	Elbphilharmonie	Hamburg, GE	Herzog & de Meuron	Warehouse	Opera house	1966/2017
Boxes	Hôtel-Dieu	Lyon, FR	AIA Life Designers + Didier Repellin	Hospital	Hotel, leisure, shopping mall	1184/2019

AR Post-functional Forms

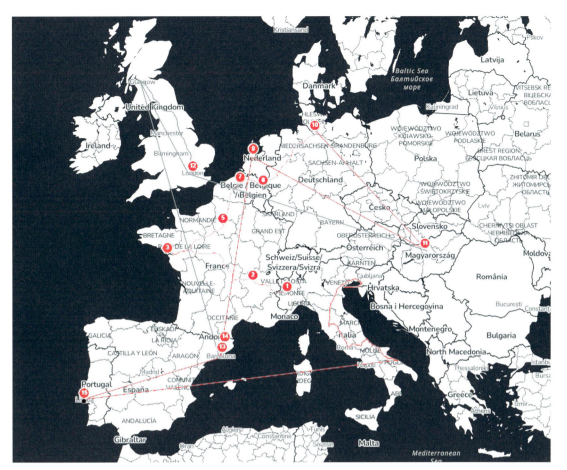

Fieldwork "Atlas of Potential".
Route of the 40-day fieldwork
to visit the 16 case studies

Route of the fieldwork.
16 Case Studies + Examples
and Unexpected

■ Case Study
● Example
○ Unexpected

Adaptive Reuse Projects Through Stages of Completeness 65

FOOTPRINTS

Footprint, noun.
The mark made by a person's or animal's foot.
 [GENERAL]
The amount of space on a surface that something needs.
 [IN ENGINEERING, ARCHITECTURE]
A measurement of the size, effect, etc. of something.
 [IN BUSINESS, ENVIRONMENT]

(Cambridge University 2024b)

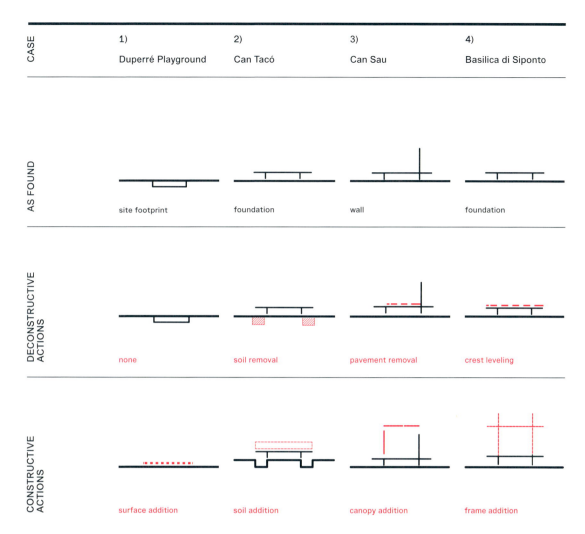

"Footprints" in terms of completeness and (de)constructive actions

This group of four projects shares a common challenge: the buildings involved have largely deteriorated due to previous demolitions or natural decay, leaving behind minimal structural remnants. The design strategy for each project focuses on these scarce remains. For example, the Duperré playground began as a vacant lot integrated into the urban landscape, while Can Taco and the Basilica di Siponto consisted only of the foundations of ancient structures. The Can Sau project offered slightly more, with a façade and a few partial walls still intact. In each case, the projects engage with the incomplete layers of "site" and "structure," interpreting their fragmented forms to breathe new life into the spaces.

Duperré Playground

Case 1

In the heart of Pigalle, in the IX arrondissement of Paris, at Rue Duperré 22, a disused parking lot has been transformed into the iconic Pigalle Duperré Court. The plot, owned by *Société Électricité de France S.A.* (EDF),[3] was previously believed to have housed a small building, later demolished to make way for the parking lot that existed until 2009.[4] The site is bordered by the *Lycée Edgar Quinet Filières Professionnelles*[5] on its west side, providing direct access to the court through a door and external stairway. Surrounding the rest of the plot are residential buildings, with an open connection to Rue Duperré on the south side.

The basketball court has undergone a process of recurring transformation from 2009 to January 2020, when the last intervention occurred. The transformation of this space began in 2007, when Stéphane Ashpool, fashion designer and founder of the sportswear brand Pigalle Paris, along with residents, convinced the district mayor to convert the parking lot into a modern sports facility. The project began as a "social experiment" to create a communal space for sports and art. In 2009, Ashpool collaborated with Nike and French-Asian artist Yué "Nyno" Wu to paint the first version of the court. Its grand opening attracted notable figures such as Michael Jordan, Scottie Pippen, Spike Lee, and LeBron James.

In 2012, to launch a new collection, Ashpool collaborated with the French design agency Ill-Studio and sportswear brand Nike to redesign the court's surfaces. The result was a visually striking court adorned with vibrant, colorful patterns, establishing the site as a global icon of urban design and adaptive reuse. The space has undergone continuous renovations, with updates in 2015, 2017, 2020, and most recently in 2024. In October 2024, the court's design shifted from a gradient of bright yellows and bold blues—previously showcased—to a linear, multicolored optical pattern symbolizing diversity and inclusion.[6]

Location	Paris, France
Function (old/new)	Parking lot / Basketball field
Year (old/adapted)	1850s[1]/ 2009-2012-2015-2017-2020-2024
Architect (original/adaptation)	N/A / Ill-Studio
Property (old/new)	Électricité de France S.A. (EDF) – The Île-de-France Region[2]/ City of Paris
Morpho-structural type (existing/addition)	Masonry / Low / S
GSA (old/new)	230 m² / 230 m²
Height (old/new)	N/A / 0-4 m
Promoter (new)	Pigalle + Nike
Cost (old/new)	Not disclosed
Decay stage	Site footprint
Basic materials (old/new)	Brick / None (rubber plaster)
Embodied energy (retroactive/new)	0 MJ/m² / + 0 MJ/m²

Duperré Playground, dimensional and morphological analysis

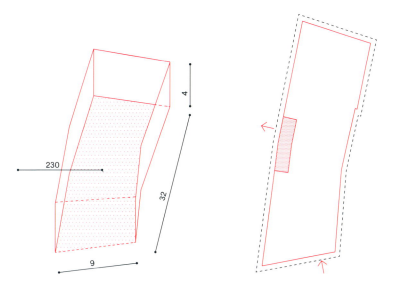

Footprints 69

Though the court closes at night, it is open daily from 10 am to 6 pm and free for public use.

This project spans approximately 230 square meters of walkable area—modest in scale yet fitting for the typical plot sizes in the area. Rather than adding new structures, adaptive reuse focuses on enhancing the existing semi-enclosed space, allowing public access from the street while defining the boundaries of the court. The plot originally featured asphalt and remnants of windows on the perimeter walls, many of which still exist in the upper sections, left untreated and unpainted. Morphologically, the open space functions like a fence, forming an enclosure on a polygonal surface, close to a rectangular shape.

The court's new surfaces are made from weather-resistant rubber composed entirely of recycled materials, provided by Nike through its Nike Grind program. The existing masonry perimeter walls have been carefully preserved, reinforcing the project's sustainability focus. With approximately 500 cubic meters of brickwork remaining intact and no new structural materials added, the embodied energy of the project is effectively zero. Additionally, using around 24 cubic meters of recycled rubber plaster for the court's surfaces and finishes significantly reduces its environmental impact, making the transformation both efficient and environmentally friendly.

Duperré Playground, basketball field in use, designed by Ill-Studio, July 2021, Paris

Can Tacó

Case 2

The archaeological site of Can Tacó is nestled in the fragmented metropolitan landscape of Turons de les Tres Creus. Originally a residential and administrative settlement linked to the Roman military governance of the region before the construction of Via Augusta, this site is now located within a natural and archaeological park. Overlooking the industrial and logistical areas of Montmeló and Montornès del Vallès, this site is now a podium that reinterprets the spatial qualities of the ancient *Domus*.

On-site archeological research began in 2003 with support from the local municipalities Montmeló and Montornès del Vallès, leading to its designation as a heritage site.[8] Toni Gironès was commissioned to design the adaptation project. In October 2021, the site was inaugurated as "Mons Observans" (Mountain of Observation). The adaptation project both preserves and enhances the Roman structures by carefully reshaping the landscape.[9] Soil from archaeological excavations, along with gravel and rocks from the original Roman quarry, already present on site, were carefully arranged to articulate the new space. Steel mesh filled with stones, earth, and gravel was used to recreate the horizontal planes once traversed by the Romans.

According to Gironès, the choice of materials reflects this duality: the locally sourced "llicorella" stone connects to the natural landscape, while the use of metal bars evokes the area's industrial heritage, symbolizing the fusion of "stone and steel, mountain and industry, in landscapes of accumulation energized by the contact between fragments."[10]

Location	Montmeló-Montornés del Vallés, Barcelona, Spain
Function (old/new)	Roman residential settlement / Archaeological site and viewpoint
Year (old/adapted)	second century BC / 2012
Architect (original/adaptation)	N/A / Toni Gironés
Property (old/new)	Ayuntamento de Montmeló i Montornés del Vallés
Morpho-structural type (existing/addition)	Masonry / Low / L
GSA (old/new)	2,500 m² / 2,500 m²
Height (old/new)	N/A / 0-1.5 m
Promoter (new)	Ayuntamento de Montmeló i Montornés del Vallés
Cost (old/new)	N/A / € 130,000 [7]
Decay stage	Foundations
Basic materials (old/new)	Llicorella stone / Llicorella stone, steel bars, rods
Embodied Eenergy (retroactive/new)	934,500 MJ (374 MJ/m²) / + 1,691,071 MJ (676 MJ/m²)

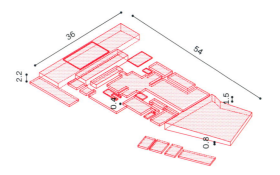

Can Tacó, dimensional and morphological analysis

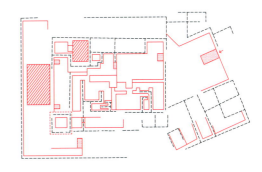

Footprints

The original building, subjected to the forces of nature and weather, gradually deteriorated over the centuries, leaving only the foundations and partial walls buried beneath layers of soil.

The ancient settlement was divided into two parts: the main building at the hilltop and the courtyards that housed rooms and service areas. The main structure served as a residential space and hosted institutional events, with its northwest side bordered by two towers.[11] The new design is closely tied to its specific topographical conditions and the preserved remnants of the existing walls. The project utilizes the remains as a foundation, reversing voids and built elements to create a system of interconnected platforms. These platforms, though connected, are physically independent and include minimal structures, such as two protective shelters and a wire sculpture. The platforms vary in height, ranging from 50 centimeters to 2 meters, and are linked by stairs and open corridors. The shelters both protect vulnerable remnants, like the main cistern and highlight the spatial arrangement of the rooms. Meanwhile, the rusted metal tube structure enhances visibility from the street and evokes one of the original towers.

The project relies on two primary materials: the locally abundant "llicorella" stone—a quartzite-rich slate characteristic of the Catalan Priorat region—and rusted steel bars. The stone, already present in piles from earlier excavations, and the steel, referencing the nearby industrial zones, are integral to the design. More than 8 cubic meters of steel bars are arranged in simple reinforcing cages, carefully positioned to avoid damaging the ancient walls. The stone is laid dry within the steel cages to form a perimeter approximately 60 centimeters thick, with finer gravel filling the gaps. The structure is reinforced with 2 steel mesh layers: the first, a grid of 15 by 15 centimeters made of 10-millimeter bars, stiffened by transverse elements for stability, and the second, a grid of 15 by 3 centimeters made of 6-millimeter bars, holding smaller gravel. The same material is used for steps, handrails, and parapets. Stell components embody almost 2,000,000 megajoules of energy, while the slate—partly excluded from calculation due to its existing presence on site—adds approximately 1,000,000 megajoules.

Can Tacó, designed by Toni Gironés, view from the top of the platform, July 2021, Montmeló

Can Sau

Case 3

Can Sau was originally a leather manufacturing factory, later acquired by the municipality and demolished in 2017, because half of the structure was affecting the new street alignment. During the demolition process, two concrete buttresses were constructed to secure the existing façade. In 2018, at the request of the Olot municipality, Un Parell d'Arquitectes were initially tasked with a modest design assignment, limited to resurfacing an area of a bit more than 100 square meters, with a budget of approximately 30,000 euros. Given the small scale of the project, the architects chose to creatively extend the neighboring house, using the budget to enhance the vertical plane and support the addition of a new roof. Rather than opting for a conventional waterproof metal cladding, as initially anticipated by the municipality, the design introduced a porous façade that not only provides a scenic backdrop to urban life but also serves as a venue for events, enriching the community space.

    The design aims to complete the existing elements, the buttresses, and the traces of domestic activity evident on the party wall. In terms of structural systems, load-bearing walls and vaults are articulating the new vaulted brick canopy supported by a red steel structure. This is due to the existing concrete buttresses, which necessitate the design of the vaults tangential to them and supported by an L-section. Two new metal pillars in an eastern vault support the existing wall in counteracting horizontal forces.

Location	Olot, Catalonia, Spain
Function (old/new)	Suitcase factory and shop / Urban void / Urban stage
Year (old/adapted)	1900s / 2017 / 2019
Architect (original/adaptation)	N/A / Un Parell d'Arquitectes[12]
Property (old/new)	Municipality of Olot
Morpho-structural type (existing/addition)	Masonry / Arch / XS / M
GSA (old/new)	113 m² / 113 m²
Height (old/new)	0 m / 10 m
Promoter (new)	Municipality of Olot
Cost (old/new)	N/A / € 30,000[13]
Decay stage	Wall
Basic materials (old/new)	Limestone bricks + concrete / hollow bricks + steel
Embodied energy (retroactive/new)	685,810 MJ (6069 MJ/m²) / + 217,484 MJ (1925 MJ/m²)

Can Sau, dimensional and morphological analysis

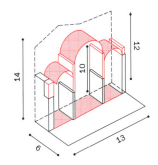 

Footprints

The project was enhanced by visual artist Quim Domene, who created glass panels to celebrate the neighborhood's history of craftsmanship and commerce, inspired by Sadurni Brunet.[14] The panels include Brunet's hydraulic floor design, two fabric patterns from the eighteenth-century local textile industry, and a glass tile pattern from a doctor's house. A transparent panel also lists the old shops of Olot's city center, preserving their memory as commercial activity since shifted.

The new structure evokes the section of Tura Church, confined between narrow streets, as well as, on a different scale, the typical chapels on the façades of the old town's buildings.

In morphological terms, the current arrangement is strongly determined by the existing scan, a configuration that repeats vaulted nooks and niches. Moreover, the small dimensions and the predominance of the vertical façade contribute to making an intervention on the vertical plane.

The new design started from a vacant lot, the main façade marked by the previous activities, two partial walls, and two central buttresses. The project preserves the effects of time on the structure; instead of erasing any trace of deterioration, it incorporates these traces into a new architecture. A few windows and doors are outlined within the new brick façade, giving the impression of a lively façade, even at night.

The existing materials of the party wall were preserved, with only unstable elements removed. Central buttresses are made of reinforced concrete, while the lateral ones are volcanic stone with lime mortar. Some fragments are solid ceramic bricks, while others are hollow ceramic bricks. The new load-bearing walls and partitions use hollow bricks with lime mortar joints. The vaults are made of brick, mortar, and waterproof paint. Steel pillars support the vaults and braces, while sandstone steps, repurposed from another site, are used beneath the vaults. The pavement consists of concrete with basalt aggregate and an acid-wash finish.

The existing structural elements contain about 686,000 megajoules of embodied energy, which is more than 6,000 megajoules per square meter. In comparison, the new structure has around 217,500 megajoules of embodied energy or about 1,930 megajoules per square meter.

Can Sau, designed by Un Parell d'Arquitectes, photo of the new structure, August 2021, Olot

Basilica di Siponto

Case 4

The intervention in the Archaeological Park of Siponto recreates and reinterprets the early Christian basilica located near the Romanesque church in Siponto, a small town near Foggia, southern Italy. Although situated along the main street and near a railway station, the site is somewhat isolated, surrounded by a low-urbanized landscape with abandoned buildings, about half an hour's drive from the highway. Edoardo Tresoldi's project is based on the remains of the basilica, originally consisting of a nave, two aisles, a central apse, and a mosaic floor. This work is part of a broader Archaeological Park project covering over 18,000 square meters, including the restoration of the nearby Basilica of Santa Maria Maggiore.

The Basilica di Siponto, originally built in the twelfth century, was abandoned after the port swamped and two violent earthquakes (in 1223 and 1255). Reconstructed three times, only its foundations remain today. In 2015, the Ministry of Cultural Heritage and Tourism (MiBACT)[16] funded Edoardo Tresoldi's art project "Dove l'arte ricostruisce il tempo." Working with a team of thirty professionals, including architects, archaeologists, and engineers, Tresoldi designed and built a new metallic structure in just five months. This installation, serving as both an artistic piece and event venue, was inaugurated in 2016. The project, costing around 900,000 euros, has since attracted approximately 8,000 visitors annually.[17]

Location	Manfredonia, Foggia, Italy
Function (old/new)	Basilica ruin / Installation, stage
Year (old/adapted)	1117 / 2016
Architect (original/adaptation)	N/A / Edoardo Tresoldi
Property (old/new)	Regione Puglia
Morpho-structural type (existing/addition)	Masonry / Arch / Frame / M / M
GSA (old/new)	820 m² / 820 m²
Height (old/new)	1 m / 14 m
Promoter (new)	Soprintendenza Beni Archeologici della Puglia, Segretariato Regionale del MiBACT per la Puglia
Cost (old/new)	€ 900,000[15]
Decay stage	Foundations
Basic materials (old/new)	Millstone grit / Concrete + steel wire
Embodied energy (retroactive/new)	737,503 MJ (899 MJ/m²) / + 1,678,295 MJ (2,047 MJ/m²)

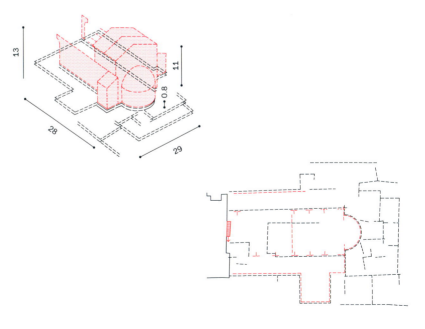

Basilica di Siponto, dimensional and morphological analysis

Footprints

According to Edoardo Tresoldi, the power of this intervention lies in its fusion of art, landscape, and history, offering a modern interpretation of restoration through contemporary art. At the time of the project, the site's materials were limited to stone foundations covering an area of about 820 square meters, with walls averaging one meter in height. Tresoldi's new structure reaches a height of 14 meters, following the original foundations without fully reconstructing the naves or roof. Instead, it suggests the tripartite layout and apse, offering a partial, intentionally incomplete reconstruction. The transparent mesh structure creates a "hologram" of the former Basilica, focusing on evoking its memory rather than replicating it. This installation bridges past and present, inviting the public to engage with the site's history and opening new possibilities for enhancing archaeological heritage.

The decay of the existing structure left only the foundation. By leveling the crest and adding a new frame, the project transforms this foundation into an "ideal frame," defining a new layout that highlights and reinterprets the original form. The structure is composed of wired meshes made from galvanized steel, assembled on site to form a potentially reversible, squared grid frame. During the construction, the artist and his team used hydraulic lifts, or cherry pickers, to position the pre-made sculpture blocks. Additionally, the crests of the walls were leveled and reinforced with concrete to provide a stable support surface.[18] The metallic mesh covers approximately 4,500 square meters and weighs 7 tons. The project used about 7 cubic meters of steel, 29 cubic meters of concrete, and 150 cubic meters of existing stone. No demolition was required, and the new additions account for about one-quarter of the original volume. The pre-existing structure contains around 738,000 megajoules of embodied energy, or about 978,000 megajoules per square meter, while the new structure incorporates approximately 1,678,000 megajoules or about 2,050 megajoules per square meter.

Basilica di Siponto, designed by Edoardo Tresoldi, photo of the frame, August 2021, Manfredonia, Foggia

STRUCTURES

Structure, noun.
The way in which the parts of a system or object are arranged or organized, or a system arranged in this way.
    [GENERAL]
Something that has been made or built from parts, especially a large building.
    [CONSTRUCTION]
An organ in the body, or part of an organ, that does a particular job.
    [ORGANISM]

(Cambridge University 2024d)

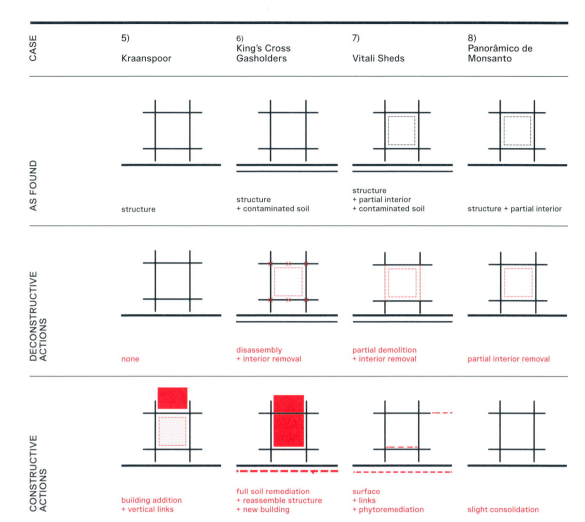

"Structures" in terms of completeness and (de)constructive actions

This group includes four projects that either rely on a structural system left behind from a planned demolition and/or a physical decline due to a process of ageing. Each project has adapted a structure from a different material basis, ensuring its reuse as infrastructure and/or with new construction grafts. The first case is the Kraanspoor, a crane in a former shipyard; the second case is the King's Cross Gasholders, large cast-iron gasholder guide frames; the third case is the Vitali Sheds, an industrial canopy in a steel thicket; and the fourth case is the Panorâmico de Monsanto, a circular frame structure in a natural park.

Structures

Kraanspoor

Case 5

Kraanspoor, which is Dutch for "craneway," is a prominent adaptive reuse project in Amsterdam's former shipyard district, Buiksloterham. Originally built in 1952 by architect JD Postma for the Nederlandsche Dok en Scheepsbouw Maatschappij (NDSM), the 270-meter-long and 9-meter-wide platform once supported cranes used in shipbuilding. Following the bankruptcy of NDSM in 1984, the area lay derelict for decades until a redevelopment competition was announced in 1999. The City of Amsterdam, eager to revitalize North Amsterdam as a cultural and creative hub, offered grants and building permits to encourage the reuse of the site.

In 2007, ING Real Estate Development commissioned OTH Architects to transform the long-dormant concrete structure into a modern office building. The new design retained the massive reinforced concrete platform, which served as the foundation for a three-story glass volume that spans the same length and extends about 14 meters wide, overhanging on both sides of the original platform. The adaptive reuse strategy included demolishing the old hoisting cranes but preserving the concrete structure, which was repurposed as storage space and fire escapes. The original space beneath the gantry was converted into archives, while the crane walkways were transformed into emergency exits.

The new glass building, with a gross volume of 40,000 cubic meters, features a steel frame, concrete slabs, and a high-tech double-skin façade. The façade varies according to sun exposure: the land-facing side has charcoal-gray dots to reduce glare and heat, while mechanized louvres regulate the incidence of sunlight. Inside, each floor offers a flexible, open-plan office space of approximately 2,700 square meters. The existing crane adds significance to the new building, which, without its connection to the pre-existing structure, could be perceived as a generic and even anonymous volume. (Guidetti and Massarente 2020) The existing platform creates the foundation for this new morphology of the "elevated box."

Location	Buiksloterham, Amsterdam, The Netherlands
Function (old/new)	Crane track / Offices
Year (old/adapted)	1952 / 2007
Architect (original/adaptation)	JD Postma / OTH Architects
Property (old/new)	ING Real Estate Development
Morpho-structural type (existing/addition)	Portal frame / M / XL / Frame / H / XXL
GSA (old/new)	2,300 m² / 12,500 m²
Height (old/new)	12 m / 26 m
Promoter (new)	ING Real Estate Development and City of Amsterdam
Cost (old/new)	€ 28 M
Decay stage	Structure
Basic materials (old/new)	Reinforced concrete / Steel + concrete
Embodied energy (retroactive/new)	30,705,293 MJ (13,350 MJMJ/m²) / + 27,245,837 MJ (2,180 MJ/m²)

Kraanspoor, dimensional and morphological analysis

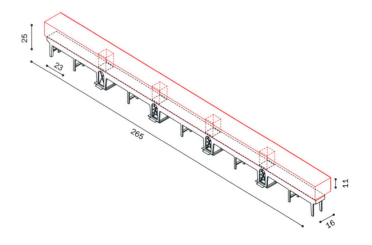

Structures

The new structure was designed to utilize the maximum allowable load of the existing platform, with lightweight materials reducing the weight by about half compared to conventional construction. Prefabricated components, including new stairways and panoramic lifts, were attached to the existing concrete portals to improve stability while preserving the original structure's aesthetic.

Kraanspoor's design cleverly separates the old and new structures, with the gap between the concrete base and the glass façade creating the illusion of the building floating above the craneway. The project was lauded for its sustainable design and construction, earning multiple awards for its energy-efficient features.[19] In addition, the inner layer of the façade opens onto a narrow buffer zone to reduce heat. (Metz 2011) The lightweight steel and concrete construction, combined with a slim "infra-floor" system, helped reduce the building's environmental impact by minimizing the need for new materials and preserving more than 4,000 cubic meters of existing reinforced concrete.

The new structure adds about one-third of the existing mass in cubic meters of materials, resulting in an embodied energy of approximately 27,000,000 megajoules. The energy impact of the original platform was around 31,000,000 megajoules, though the energy from the non-structural glass façade, about 12,000,000 megajoules, was not included in these calculations. Kraanspoor's distinctive rectangular grid layout, supported by 22 reinforced concrete portals, offers a versatile interior space for a variety of uses. The structure also features four vertical distribution systems for easy access throughout the building. The project's total cost was approximately 28 million euros, and it has since become a symbol of the successful redevelopment of North Amsterdam, contributing to the area's transformation into a vibrant cultural and creative hub under the management of the NDSM-Werf Foundation.

Kraanspoor, designed by OTH Architects, northern view, August 2021, Amsterdam

King's Cross Gasholders

Case 6

King's Cross Gasholders, also known as the Triplet, were disassembled, restored, relocated, and re-erected at the west side of St. Pancreas station with the infill of a new luxury residential complex. In 2002, in the context of the King's Cross urban redevelopment scheme, the largest in Europe, WilkinsonEyre won the design competition for three residential buildings within the existing cast iron frames, listed in the historical heritage of the UK as Nos. 10, 11, and 12 respectively.[21] This project is part of developer Argent's 27-hectare King's Cross complex.[22]

Initially, the Triplet, designed by John Clark, were erected at Goods Way (west side), King's Cross, between 1879 and 1880. Each guide frame shares a column with its neighbor, making them unique since no other co-joined gasholders were ever developed.

In 2001, the structures were disassembled and relocated to accommodate the construction of the Channel Tunnel Rail Link. The components were temporarily stored near Gasholder 8 on Goods Way (east side) before being transported to South Yorkshire for restoration by Shepley Engineers Ltd.[23]

The restored iron frames were reassembled around the new blocks, 300 meters from their original site. The new complex, inaugurated in 2008, features three cylindrical drums of accommodation at varying heights, creating a circular void at their intersection to form an open courtyard. The project includes luxury residences with 145 units, ranging from studios to three-bedroom apartments and penthouses. Shared amenities include an indoor garden, a business suite, a cocktail bar in the lobby, and a spa on the ground floor of Gasholder No. 10, with a gym and screening room on the second floor.[24]

Location	London, United Kingdom
Function (old/new)	Gasholders / Residential + office
Year (old/adapted)	1867 / 2018
Architect (original/adaptation)	John Clark / WilkinsonEyre + Arup engineers + Jonathan Tuckey Design
Property (old/new)	Argent
Morpho-structural type (existing/addition)	Frame / H / XL / Frame / H / XXL
GSA (old/new)	3,920 m² / 23,950 m²
Height (old/new)	30 m / 40.5 m
Promoter (new)	Argent[20]
Cost (old/new)	N/A / € 3.5 bn
Decay stage	Structure (contaminated soil)
Basic materials (old/new)	Cast iron / Reinforced concrete
Embodied energy (retroactive/new)	155,656,760 (39,708 MJ/m²) / + 55,063,260 MJ (2,299 MJ/m²)

King's Cross Gasholders, dimensional and morphological analysis

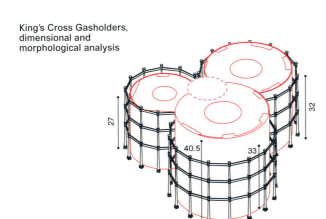
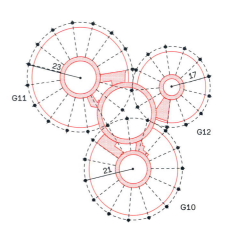

Structures

The existing frames, with diameters ranging from nearly 30 to over 45 meters, are interconnected by shared perimeter columns. A fourth circular void, approximately 25 meters wide, creates a central space between the structures. The floors within each frame are divided into segments that radiate from a central axial atrium, aligning with the original Victorian columns. Each level features a circular balcony walkway encircling the atrium, offering views of the courtyard below, while these inner atria provide access to the residences.

The new construction features sleek dark gray aluminum panels, which are complemented by recessed windows and balconies.

Gasholder No. 11 rises to more than 40 meters and consists of 12 stories, making it the tallest structure and the only one exceeding the ironwork frame. The other two buildings reach heights of 31 meters with 9 stories and 27 meters with 8 stories, reflecting the original "telescopic" gasholders that moved on vertical rails.

These new buildings are structurally independent, transferring no loads to the existing frame; however, attachment bolts at the base of the Victorian cast-iron columns are anchored to the ground floor slab. The three towers share a common basement, and the overall structure is primarily composed of reinforced concrete in a composite design, including walls, pillars, and a foundation slab supported by piles.

The new design maintains the circular morphology of the frame, organizing the residential units in slices around the circular corridors, with stair systems strategically positioned at the intersections between the blocks and the inner courtyard. Dimensionally, the new addition is more than 1,000 percent more than the existing one, considering the cubic meters of construction materials involved in the old and new structures. The volume of iron used amounts to approximately 620 cubic meters,[25] embodying around 156,000,000 megajoules of energy. Additionally, the new structure consists of about 7,700 cubic meters of reinforced concrete and 15 cubic meters of steel, which together embody over 55,000,000 megajoules. The existing structure embodied three times the energy of the new one.

King's Cross Gasholders, designed by WilkinsonEyre, exterior view, December 2022, London

Vitali Sheds

Case 7

The former industrial zone in northern Turin was transformed into Parco Dora in 2011, covering about 456,000 square meters. This redevelopment involved the partial demolition of old warehouses, including the Vitali Factory. The process started in 2004, following an international competition won by Peter Latz's team, creating a park that seamlessly blends natural spaces with functional facilities while honoring its industrial heritage. Here, we focus on the transformation of the Vitali Sheds, which consists of two connected sheds, A and B, arranged parallel to Corso Mortara.[29]

The sheds were built in 1973, but the site's industrial history dates back to the 1920s. The plant was part of the Ferriere Fiat steelworks, covering around 90,000 square meters and producing ingots for semi-finished products like sheets, pipes, and springs. It was abandoned in 1992 and officially closed in 2001. Due to significant pollution from hexavalent chromium, remediation efforts have been undertaken, with ongoing monitoring to keep contamination levels below the risk threshold.[30]

Peter Latz's project preserved the roof of the smaller Vitali Steelworks shed (A), now called Skatepark. This structure spans about 12,000 square meters and stands around 24 meters high. In contrast, the larger shed (B), covering roughly 23,500 square meters, had its roof removed, leaving concrete settling tanks, a perimeter wall, and towering steel pillars about 25 meters tall. Shed B has been transformed into a garden with flowerbeds, play areas, and pathways, linked by a raised walkway to the Ingest area, accessible via stairs and elevators in the old concrete towers.

Location	Parco Dora, Turin, Italy
Function (old/new)	Steel factory / Park, skatepark, playground
Year (old/adapted)	1973 / 2011
Architect (original/adaptation)	N/A / Latz + Partners[26]
Property (old/new)	Cassa Depositi e Prestiti (CDP)
Morpho-structural type (existing/addition)	Frame + Space frame / H / XXL
GSA[27] (old/new)	36,160 m²
Height[28] (old/new)	35 m
Promoter (new)	City of Turin + State
Cost (old/new)	N/A / € 17.2 M
Decay stage	Structure + partial interior (contaminated soil)
Basic materials (old/new)	Steel + concrete / Steel
Embodied energy (retroactive/new)	745,208,436 MJ (20,609 MJ/m²) / - 568,484,280 MJ (24,170 MJ/m²) / + 5,553,148 MJ (236 MJ/m²)

Vitali Sheds, dimensional and morphological analysis

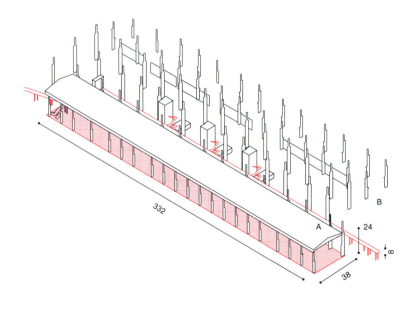
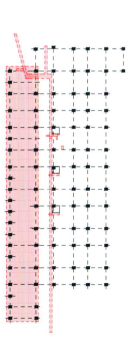

Structures

Skatepark is a massive canopy that serves as a multifunctional space for free play, events, and sports, featuring amenities like a skatepark, which inspired its new name. The venue hosts various events, including the Kappa Future Festival, attracting around 50,000 visitors annually, and the Eid al-Fitr celebration, drawing about 30,000 people each year. The area is continually evolving through minimal interventions, with the latest renovation of the skatepark completed in 2021.

Both buildings are structurally stable, with their pillars functioning independently from the outer walls. The steel structures have been cleaned and treated, maintaining an unpolished surface that showcases their authenticity. Nature has intertwined with the steel, as climbing plants gradually take over, creating an "industrial thicket" atmosphere. The preserved shed acts as a canopy over a vast area of roughly 36,000 square meters and stands about 25 meters tall, allowing for various activities requiring large covered spaces.

Building A remains a steel canopy supported by 35 pillars, while Building B retains only its pillars and concrete towers, which house stairwells. A minimalist walkway, about 130 meters long and 2 meters wide, connects the remaining concrete blocks, weaving between the pillars. The grid of pillars organizes the adjacent rectangular spaces, forming a continuous open canopy with a single aisle.

Focusing on stripping building (A) and excluding interior demolitions, no changes in cubic volume occurred during the adaptation phase. However, in the larger building (B), only the pillars, concrete towers, and a few perimeter walls remained. Approximately 2,972 cubic meters of steel are still in place in Shed A, while in Shed B, over 2,500 cubic meters of steel were dismantled, with about 361 cubic meters preserved, along with 2,030 cubic meters of reinforced concrete. Additionally, the new walkway and pillars add 25 cubic meters of steel.

In terms of embodied energy, the values are huge. Structure A boasts an impressive 652,000,000 megajoules, all conserved on site. Shed B, on the other hand, has an embodied energy of approximately 92,000,000 megajoules, or 3,945 megajoules per square meter, reflecting a significant loss of 568,000,000 megajoules during demolition.[31]

The embodied energy impact from the additions made through adaptive reuse is relatively low, totaling approximately 5,500,000 megajoules, or about 230 megajoules per square meter.

Vitali Sheds, designed by Latz and Partners, view into the Skatepark shed, June 2021, Turin

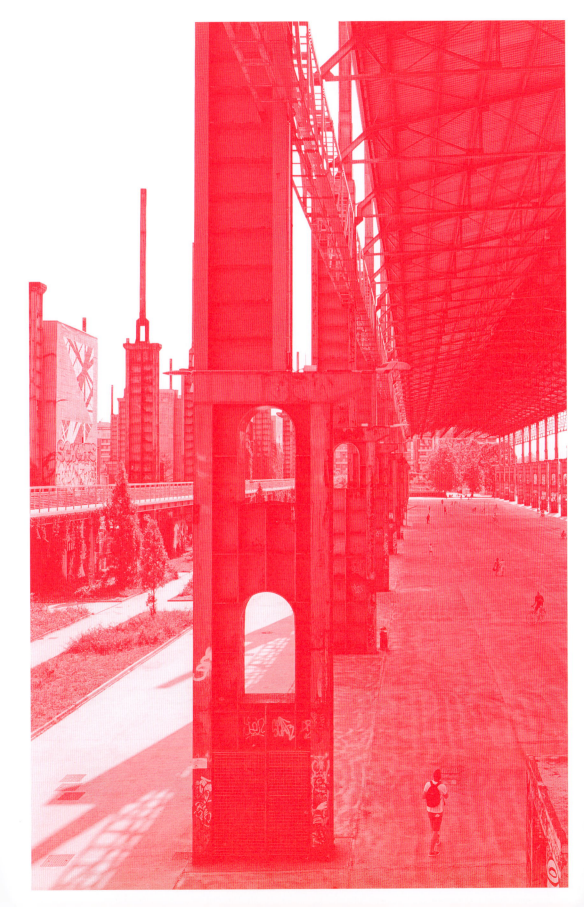

Panorâmico de Monsanto

Case 8

The Panorâmico, located in Monsanto Natural Park—Lisbon's largest green area, offers a sweeping 270-degree view of the city, the Tejo River, and the Atlantic Ocean. Designed by architect Chaves Costa and completed in 1967 as a luxury restaurant, it showcased remarkable art, including a mural by Luís Dourdil, a tile panel by Manuela Ribeiro Soares depicting pre-1755 Lisbon, and a granite bas-relief by sculptor Maria Teresa Quirino da Fonseca.

After intermittent use, the building underwent significant renovations in 1984, overseen by architect Miguel Esteves. The structure was expanded by nearly half, adding two floors. The luxurious Grão-Mestre restaurant could host about 300 guests and featured a stage and dance floor, while the Templários restaurant below seated approximately 250 guests with a terrace and balcony. The complex also included a bingo hall for 650 players and parking for 1,000 cars. The renovation cost around 2.5 million euros. (Figueiredo and Martins 2018)

Despite this transformation, the Panorâmico only operated for two years and was then used occasionally until 2001. Its remote location, far from the city center and public transport, led to a decline in public interest. From 2001 to 2007, the building reverted to the ownership of the Municipal Chamber of Lisbon, which explored various uses. However, it remained largely abandoned until 2017, when the city cleaned up the site to open it as a municipal viewpoint. The building was stripped down to its concrete frame, with stairways repaired and glass and waste removed. The city considers this reuse a temporary solution, awaiting funding for a future project. Refurbishing the Panorâmico would cost around 20 million euros, but the local government and project developers have differing opinions on the plans.

Location	Monsanto Natural Park, Lisbon, Portugal
Function (old/new)	Restaurant / Public viewpoint
Year (old/adapted)	1967 / 1984 / 2017 / ongoing
Architect (original/adaptation)	Chaves Costa / Miguel Esteves / Technical Office of the Municipality of Lisbon
Property (old/new)	Camara Municipal de Lisboa (CML)
Morpho-structural type (existing/addition)	Frame / High / XXL
GSA (old/new)	7,400 m² / 7,400 m²
Height (old/new)	26.5 m / 26.5 m
Promoter (new)	Municipality of Lisbon (CML)
Cost (old/new)	€ 2.5 M / Not disclosed
Decay stage	Structure + partial interior
Basic materials (old/new)	Reinforced concrete
Embodied energy (retroactive/new)	61,992,000 MJ (8,377 MJ/m²) / 0 MJ (0 MJ/m²)

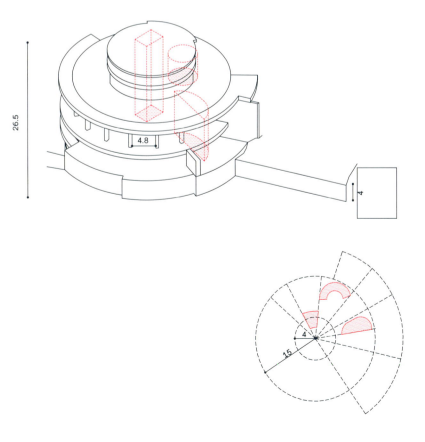

Panorâmico de Monsanto, dimensional and morphological analysis

Structures

Since 2017, the "Iminente Festival" has drawn over 5,000 visitors in just one week, and the viewpoint sees an average of about 100 visitors daily. The building's architecture features overlapping cylindrical plates, organized around two concentric spaces defined by rings of pillars. The ground floor is partly underground, and there are two main stair systems for access.

The seven-story building is organized by three stair systems, one dedicated to service use. Its gross surface area (GSA) is approximately 7,400 square meters. The circular reinforced concrete structure extends over a radius of 15 to 16 meters and reaches a height of nearly 27 meters.

In 2016, the roof was found to be damaged, prompting temporary reinforcements to preserve the original structure. Inside, some of the mosaic tiles and decorations remain intact, though the walls are mostly bare concrete, now covered with graffiti. The adaptive reuse focused on securing the structure, removing non-structural elements, and maintaining safety and access. No new structural elements or systems were added, preserving the building's original reinforced concrete skeleton from the 1984 extension. This structure contains around 9,500 cubic meters of reinforced concrete, holding an embodied energy of more than 6,000,000 megajoules. Per square meter, this accounts for roughly 8,000 megajoules. The future of the Panorâmico remains under debate. In June 2023, the municipality once again closed the site, implementing 24/7 surveillance to prevent further vandalism and protect this important piece of city heritage. As of now, the Panorâmico appears to be temporarily closed again, with new plans for its development underway. In 2024, a study was conducted by the Municipality of Lisbon to assess the building's structural safety, economic feasibility, and potential conversion for municipal use.

The study confirmed the viability of restoring the Panorâmico. However, it highlighted the need for structural reinforcement in some areas and a complete renovation of certain elements, particularly the canopy over the old restaurant. According to Ângelo Pereira, Lisbon's Green Structure Councilor, the estimated cost for the structural reinforcement and consolidation alone is approximately 10 million euros. In addition, a comprehensive restoration, including architectural interventions, is projected to cost another 13 million euros.[32] This building's temporary adaptation (2017–2023) tells us the story of temporary uses as a way of adaptive reuse.

Panorâmico de Monsanto, exterior view, August 2021, Lisbon

SHELLS

Shell, noun.
The hard outer covering of something, especially nuts, eggs, and some animals.
    [GENERAL]
The basic outer structure of a building or vehicle, especially when the parts inside have been destroyed or taken or have not yet been made.
    [CONSTRUCTION]
A company that is used to hide illegal activities.
    [ECONOMY]

(Cambridge University 2024c)

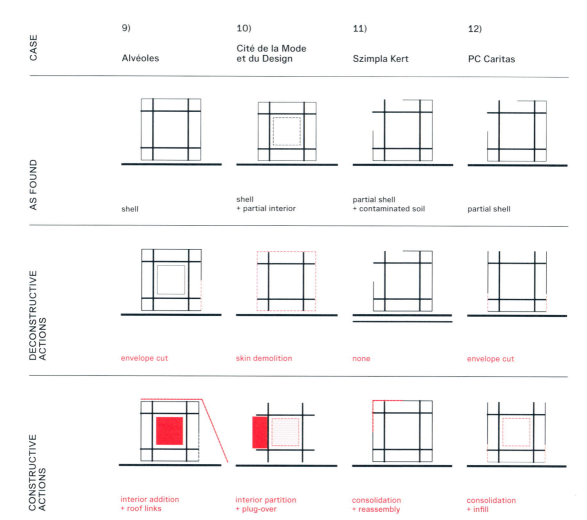

"Shells" in terms of completeness and (de)constructive actions

This group comprises four architectural projects in which the existing structure—both the envelope and roof—defines the boundary between interior and exterior spaces, sometimes creating hybrid zones. Each project starts with a shell at varying stages of completion, transforming it to allow for its reuse as either entirely or partially enclosed spaces. This is achieved through the addition of new volumes or by subdividing the existing structure. The first project, Alvéoles, adapts a former submarine military base that cannot be demolished. The second, Cité de la Mode et du Design, is the adaptation of a large industrial skeleton along the Seine River. The third, Szimpla Kert, repurposes a derelict inner-city factory, while the fourth, PC Caritas, deals with a partially demolished building, part of a psychiatric center in the countryside.

Alvéoles

Case 9

The Saint-Nazaire submarine base, one of five built by the Nazis along the Atlantic coast during World War II, has been gradually transformed into a cultural center.[34] Through several phases, the focus has been on integrating the structure with the city and re-purposing it for public and cultural activities.

The base opened in 1942 and housed U-boats, offices, and workshops until the war ended in 1945. This structure, standing approximately 18 meters tall and made from nearly 500,000 cubic meters of concrete, is one of Europe's largest bunkers. Spanning almost 4 hectares and over 100 meters in length (more than three football fields), its roof is more than 9 meters thick. The base is divided into 17 cells, or "Alvéoles," which served as submarine docks and workshops, connected by a 5-meter-wide service corridor. Despite heavy Allied bombings that destroyed much of Saint-Nazaire, the base survived intact.

After WWII, by the 1950s, the base was largely abandoned. In 1987, the French submarine S-637 Espadon was placed in the base and opened to visitors. A decade later, the City of Saint-Nazaire, with support from the government and the EU, began transforming the site into a cultural space. The transformation of the Saint-Nazaire submarine base into a cultural center took place in four main stages. Firstly, between 1996 and 2002,[35] as part of the Ville-Port project by Manuel de Solà-Morales, four aisles were opened to create views of the estuary and an exhibition center on transatlantic liners. A ramp, made of four parallel metal beams, was added to provide roof access, offering city-wide views. This ramp extends more than 50 meters over the street, connecting the roof with the city. (de Solá-Morales 2008, 38)

Secondly, in 2003, LIN Architects won the competition held by the City of Saint-Nazaire by proposing to convert Alveole-14 into a cultural center, featuring event halls and music venues in the former workshop. The project focused on four key elements: a space for emerging arts (LiFE), a venue for music events, recording studios (VIP), enhancing the main corridor ("the street"), and adding the "Radome" on the rooftop.[36]

Location	Saint-Nazaire, France
Function (old/new)	Submarine base / Cultural center, museum
Year (old/adapted)	1942 / 2002 / 2011 / 2014 / 2018
Architect (original/adaptation)	Albert Speer / Manuel de Sola Moralès / Gilles Clément + Coloco / LIN Finn Geipel + Giulia Andi, 51N4E + Bourbouze et Graindorge
Property (old/new)	French Navy / Municipality of Saint-Nazaire
Morpho-structural type (existing/addition)	Frame + shear walls + space frame / M / XXL
GSA (old/new)	39,000 m² / 39,000 m²
Height (old/new)	18 m / 18 m
Promoter (new)	City of Saint Nazaire + European Union + Le Lieu Unique for Estuaire 2009-2011
Cost[33] (old/new)	N/A / € 13 M / € 7.1 M / € 5.9 M
Decay stage	Shell + interior
Basic materials (old/new)	Highly reinforced concrete / Steel, LVL
Embodied energy (retroactive/new)	14,280,000,000 MJ (366,154 MJ/m²) / - 43,137,500 MJ (1,106 MJ/m²) / 52,786,524 MJ (1,354 MJ/m²)

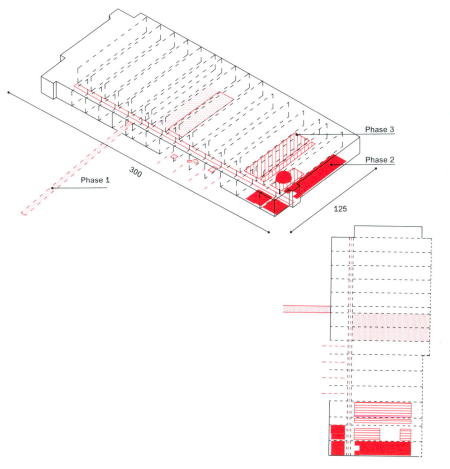

Saint-Nazaire base, dimensional and morphological analysis

The VIP venue, designed as a black box for contemporary music, accommodates 600 people and includes recording studios and technical walkways. The LiFE space occupies the former submarine basin, measuring approximately 91 meters by 20 meters, with a height of 18 meters. It features a corrugated metal ceiling, scenic walkways, and a bar overlooking the double-height area. A 15-meter-wide folding door opens directly onto the harbor. Visitors access the hall from the landward side via the former service corridor, which also leads to the bunker roof through a steel staircase with 27 steps. Thirdly, the roof was cut open to allow access to the roof, where the newly installed 9-meter-high dome, illuminated at night, makes internal changes visible. (LIN Architects 2007; Lecardane and Tesoriere 2011) In 2011, Gilles Clément with Coloco designed the "Jardins du Tiers Paysage" on the rooftop, featuring native plant species from the estuary in three sections: the central wooded area where beams cover the submarine chambers, a central section on either side of a narrow canal, and a rectangular garden near the dome. (COLOCO 2011)[37]

To conclude, in 2018, studio 51N4E led the conversion of Alvéole-12 into a multi-event hall featuring a long space with a permanent stage and a terrace overlooking the bay. This area includes artist facilities, such as lodges and cloakrooms, while Alvéole-13 was transformed into co-working spaces, warehouses, and permanent stands.

Despite sustaining damage from wartime bombings, the base has remained structurally sound, making demolition financially unfeasible for a city still recovering from the war. As a result, the base continues to evolve and adapt, serving various functions, including as a COVID-19 vaccination hub from 2021 to 2022.

The building's design resembles a "clustered slab," characterized by a broad layout that organizes repeated spaces in a linear sequence. It effectively connects the urban environment to the surrounding landscape through walkways and roof openings that face the port. (Guidetti and Massarente 2021)

The original structure is made of heavily reinforced concrete, while recent additions use lighter materials like steel for walkways and platforms and laminated veneer lumber for portals in Alvéole 12 and 12bis. These new materials account for just 0.07% of the building's total mass, with displaced concrete at approximately 0.3%. The energy embodied in the original materials is significantly higher, exceeding 14 billion megajoules in the concrete, while the newer adaptations contribute only around 50,000,000 megajoules.

Saint-Nazaire base, view from the port, July 2021, Saint-Nazaire

Cité de la Mode et du Design

Case 10

Les Docks Magasins, designed by Georges Morin-Goustiaux and built in 1907, are among the oldest reinforced concrete buildings in Paris. Located at Quai d'Austerlitz, they were converted into customs warehouses in 1915 for the transfer of goods. By the 1980s, the site mainly served as a carpet warehouse and examination facility before being abandoned in 1984.

As part of the *Rive Gauche* project launched in 2004 by the City and the Port of Paris, the design by Jakob & MacFarlane was selected for the conversion of this structure. Completed in 2009, the new building houses the *Institut Français de la Mode*, a contemporary art museum, restaurants, and bookstores. Since 2013, it has also been home to the Musée d'Art Ludique. (Barasch 2019, 136–41)

The adaptive intervention preserved the existing structure while wrapping a glass skin around it. The original reinforced concrete structure is approximately 280 meters long and 39 meters deep, covering around 12,000 square meters. Transshipment platforms near the Seine were demolished to meet technological needs and reinforce the existing structure. (Destombes 2017)

The original three-story design included four pavilions, each about 10 meters wide and 7.5 meters long. On the ground floor, the bay remains accessible for storing and loading materials.

The new building features various spaces across three levels. The partially underground area, called Le Quai (the Platform), measures about 1,200 square meters and can accommodate around 1,000 attendees for cultural events. The ground floor houses the Institut Français de la Mode—2,200 square meters—and rental spaces like the *Galerie d'actualité*. The first floor contains the 3,400-square-meter Gran Foyer, which is divisible into three sections for up to 2,500 people. The rooftop, affording a view of the Seine, spans about 600 square meters and offers a bar and café that can cater for around 500 guests during outdoor events.

Location	Paris, France
Function (old/new)	Industrial Warehouse / Cultural center Cité de la Mode et du Design
Year (old/adapted)	1907 / 2009
Architect (original/adaptation)	George Morin-Goustiaux / Jakob + MacFarlane
Property (old/new)	Port of Paris / City of Paris
Morpho-structural type (existing/addition)	Frame / Space Frame / M / H / XXL
GSA (old/new)	12,000 m² / 15,000 m²
Height (old/new)	16 m / 21 m
Promoter (new)	Caisse des Dépôts + French Institute of Fashion
Cost[39] (old/new)	N/A / € 47.5 M
Decay stage	Shell + partial interior
Basic materials (old/new)	Reinforced concrete / Steel
Embodied energy (retroactive/new)	131,931,576 MJ (10,994 MJ/m²) / 52,239,096 MJ (3,483 MJ/m²)

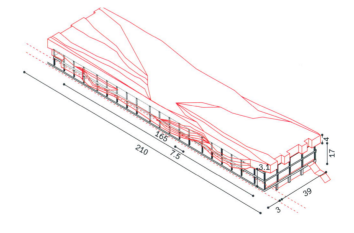
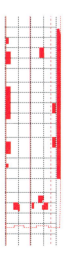

Cité de la Mode et du Design, dimensional and morphological analysis

Shells

New structural elements made of vividly painted steel contrast with the concrete frame. The lower platform level serves as an open space, with a few metal grids regulating access. The existing volume comprises two blocks connected by a central atrium, with a steel "plug-over" creating a covered passageway around 320 meters long that links to the quay. This design consolidates traffic at the front and transforms the roof into a usable terrace, providing a view of the river and attracting around 1.5 million visitors annually. The total cost of this adaptive reuse intervention was approximately 47.5 million euros.

The framework of beams and pillars is preserved, and the steel and glass skin wraps the existing frame while facilitating circulation. The interior is organized around a central void, integrating the ground floor with the riverside path.

To create the "plug-over" design, the architects divided the building's repetitive structural rhythm into four parts, each about 8 meters wide, separated by 10-meter spans. The original structure was robust, weighing around 330 tons, although some column-to-beam connections were less stable.

The plug-over incorporates a series of vertical slices with gantry frames made from steel tubes with a diameter of 17 centimeters, suspended at 2.5-meter intervals from the building's new top edge beam. This vertical load distribution allows the plug-over to withstand side winds and dead loads against the lower floor plates. The ends of the portal arches maintain curvature through vertical steel support tubes acting in tension, with smaller tubes with a 10-centimeter diameter added for wind truss stability.

The project features 630 glass panels, requiring careful parametric modeling for cost efficiency. The structure needed to be consolidated due to concrete deterioration but remains a raw, regular frame, enabling modular division and additional features like the stair system. Morphologically, the buildings act as a grid block, allowing infinite modularity and the potential for large, open spaces.

Interior additions are not considered part of the essential structural system for energy calculations. These composite materials account for almost 1,700 cubic meters, while glass is around 50 cubic meters, and timber for the roof deck and stairs is about 80 cubic meters. Overall, the structural addition embeds around 52,000,000 megajoules of energy, while the energy in the old concrete bulk is more than 130,000,000 megajoules.

Cité de la Mode et du Design, designed by Jakob + MacFarlane, view from the Seine River, July 2021, Paris

Szimpla Kert

Case 11

Since 1841, this building has stood on Kazinczy Street in Budapest's VII district. Originally a residential building, it later became a factory and eventually a cultural center. The Pokorny family owned the property from 1829 to 1898, constructing the U-shaped house in 1841 after a flood destroyed the original. An upper floor was added in 1873 by Janos Pokorny. (Perczel and Lábass 2007, 187)

In 1911, Sandor Heber purchased the building and turned it into a stove factory. During WWII, the Nazi regime confiscated all Jewish-owned properties, including the Herber family's. Under communism, the factory was nationalized and used to produce small metal components, most likely bullets.[42] Abandoned and in ruins since the 1980s, the building was slated for demolition by local authorities and sold in 1990. However, in 1994, the capital city authority extended protection to include the façade, thus preventing its demolition. Nevertheless, the former owner began demolishing the interior while preserving the façade, intending to turn the site into a parking lot until land values rose. The neighboring orthodox community had also shown interest in purchasing the land to demolish the entire building and construct a Mikveh, a Jewish ritual bath, according to current manager Ábel Zsendovits.

By 2004, half of the original masonry structure remained, with demolition debris filling the gutted rooms and only electricity still functioning. In 2006, four entrepreneurs, led by Zsendovits, transformed the site into Szimpla Kert, opening a pub and an open-air cinema in the courtyard of the partially demolished building. Over the next 15 years, they undertook significant repairs, including structural consolidation, reassembling the second floor, installing necessary systems, and constructing a covered terrace—all primarily using materials salvaged from the previous demolition. In 2020, they renovated the leaking roof and added an elevated walkway.[43]

Location	Budapest, Hungary
Function (old/new)	Residential / Factory / Ruin pub
Year (old/adapted)	1841 / 1911 / 2014
Architect (original/adaptation)	N/A / None
Property[40] (old/new)	Private
Morpho-structural type (existing/addition)	Masonry / High / XXL
GSA (old/new)	1,500 m² / 2,000 m²
Height[41] (old/new)	12 m / 12 m
Promoter (new)	Szimpla Kert Association
Cost (old/new)	N/A / Not disclosed
Decay stage	Partial shell
Basic materials (old/new)	Brick, concrete / Brick, concrete, steel, timber
Embodied energy (retroactive/new)	946,512 MJ (631 MJ/m²) / 795,116 MJ (398 MJ/m²)

Szimpla Kert,
dimensional and
morphological analysis

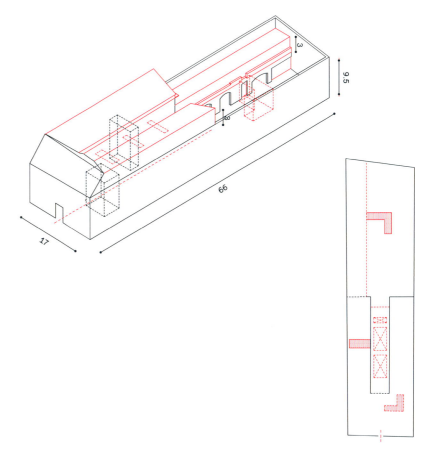

Shells 113

Szimpla Kert's adaptive reuse of this ruin became a model for successful regeneration projects throughout Budapest. Today, Szimpla Kert is not just a pub but a vibrant cultural hub, hosting music events, art exhibitions, and a Sunday farmer's market featuring local produce. By 2019, the venue welcomed around 2 million visitors annually.[44]

The restaurant operated until its closure in March 2020 due to the COVID-19 pandemic. Despite some decay, key elements like the façade, roof, and interior partitions were preserved. Before its adaptive reuse, the building was a partially demolished shell with structural issues. New features, including stairs, a covered terrace, and essential systems, were added, while the building's deteriorated appearance, characterized by overlapping layers of plaster, enhances its identity as a ruin pub.

The structure features a central entrance on Kazinczy Street and consists of two symmetrical wings, each about 30 meters long and 7 meters wide. A partially covered hallway leads to a courtyard, and a semi-demolished wing is topped with a terrace enclosed by a greenhouse-like structure. The building has two to three above-ground levels, with offices in the attic and a vaulted basement for storage. Public access is limited to the first and second floors, which are connected by overhead walkways and small terraces added during renovations.

Circulation is managed by two original stairwells and an additional one leading to the terrace, created during the 2014 adaptive reuse project, which was largely self-organized by the management to accommodate increased tourism. The building incorporates bricks, steel, and concrete, with timber added during the roof renovations. Inside, eclectic furnishings, including a dentist's chair and a bathtub, create a whimsical "cabinet of curiosities" atmosphere.

Since the start of adaptive reuse, no further demolition has occurred, and additions now make up roughly 11 percent of the original structure. The adaptation added 500 square meters, bringing the total to around 2,000 square meters. In energy terms, the new concrete and steel contribute about 800,000 megajoules, while the existing bricks and concrete account for nearly 1,000,000 megajoules.

Szimpla Kert, view from Kazinczy street, July 2021, Budapest

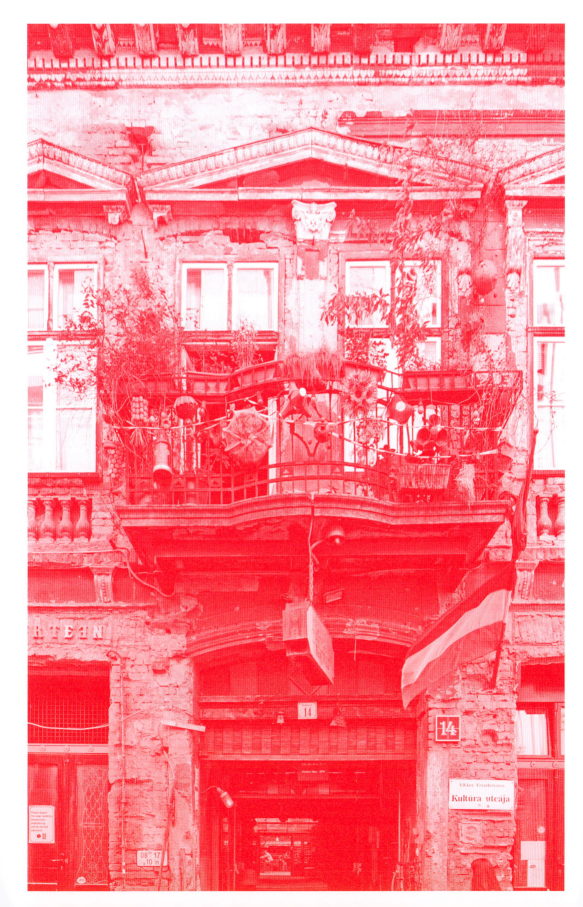

PC Caritas

Case 12

The Sint Jozef Building is part of the Melle Psychiatric Center near Ghent. Originally, the mental clinic comprised several distinct structures set amidst gardens, including the Saint Jozef Villa. This historical building has been transformed into the Kanunnik Triest Plein (PC Caritas), featuring a treatment room, conference area, event venue, café, and forum. It now serves as a "plaza" for patients, staff, visitors, and residents, providing a space for breaks, evening meetings, and passersby heading to the hospital cafeteria.

Constructed in 1908, the original building was largely dismantled in 2014 and adapted by DVVT Architects in 2016. Many villas fell into disrepair, and the Sint Jozef Building was initially slated for demolition in 2014. However, delays due to asbestos cleanup left its future uncertain. Meanwhile, the research collective BAVO coordinated workshops with therapists and residents to create an architectural design brief aimed at integrating the ruins into the surrounding park. This led to the halt of demolition, and BAVO's findings were presented to DVVT Architects, who planned to preserve the building in its largely demolished state, following a principle of minimal intervention. All mineral materials on the ground surface were removed, and the floor was rebuilt with stones to facilitate water drainage. The antique fireplace was preserved in its original form, and windows were lowered to allow for all-directional openings. The basement was transformed into an auditorium, and a tree was planted. The only new additions include a white loggia reminiscent of old villas and greenhouses that provides extra rooms. This initiative emphasizes enhancing the existing shell rather than constructing new structures or restoring the building to its original state. (De Vylder et al. 2018)

Location	Melle, Ghent, Belgium
Function (old/new)	Psychiatric healthcare / Meeting room, square
Year (old/adapted)	1908 / 2016
Architect (original/adaptation)	N/A / Architecten de Vylder Vinck Taillieu (DVVT Architects) + BAVO Studio
Property (old/new)	Karus
Morpho-structural type (existing/addition)	Masonry / High / L
GSA (old/new)	1,800 m² / 1,800 m²
Height (old/new)	15 m / 15 m
Promoter (new)	Karus
Cost (old/new)	N/A / € 475,000
Decay stage	Partial shell
Basic materials (old/new)	Brick + wood / Steel + brick
Embodied energy (retroactive/new)	6,713,333 MJ (3,730 MJ/m²) / - 131,443 MJ (73 MJ/m²) / 1,850,328 MJ (1,028MJ/m²)

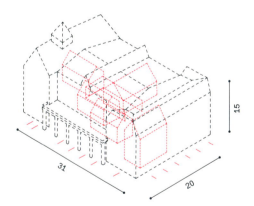

PC Caritas, dimensional and morphological analysis

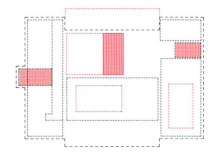

Shells

Instead of reconstruction, the half-destroyed structure underwent repairs. Original materials—brick, timber, and concrete—were preserved, with lost bricks replaced by concrete blocks. Removed windows were rebuilt using reinforced concrete and basic formwork. To enhance structural integrity, a few new green-painted steel profiles were added as load-bearing components. The design introduces an openable and configurable dollhouse concept, while traces of surface degradation, such as peeling paint and rusted greenhouse features, remain visible on the additions. (Fitz et al. 2019; Devoldere et al. 2023)

The remodeling project cost less than 500,000 euros, 300,000 of which came from the original demolition budget. (Kleilein 2018) Compliance with safety requirements has been challenged many times.[45] This structure functions as a temporary storage facility for materials and allows for potential future expansions. Previously, it was a semi-gutted shell undergoing demolition.

The building consists of four levels: a newly opened basement, a ground floor serving as an open square, and two upper stories. With a rectangular layout of approximately 30 meters wide, 20 meters long, and 15 meters high, it covers around 1,800 square meters. The conversion of windows into doors has created multiple entry points on each side. Vertical circulation is facilitated by two stairwells at opposite ends, with a new staircase providing access to the basement.

Inside, there are five enclosed chambers, each designed as a miniature greenhouse, and a sixth chamber that spans two levels from the ground floor. In terms of materials, about 16 cubic meters were demolished, 870 cubic meters were preserved, and 52 cubic meters were added, resulting in 8 percent of the structure being newly added and 2 percent demolished. The primary existing material is brick, while the additions consist mainly of steel beams. The embodied energy for this adaptive reuse intervention is approximately 2,000,000 megajoules, compared to about 7,000,000 megajoules for the historical building.

PC Caritas, designed by DVVT Architects, interior view from the basement, July 2021, Melle, Ghent

BOXES

Box, noun.
A square or rectangular container with stiff sides and sometimes a lid.
    [GENERAL]
A (small) place with walls.
    [CONSTRUCTION]
Any square or rectangular space on a form, sports field, road, etc., separated from the main area by lines.
    [SPORT]

(Cambridge University 2024a)

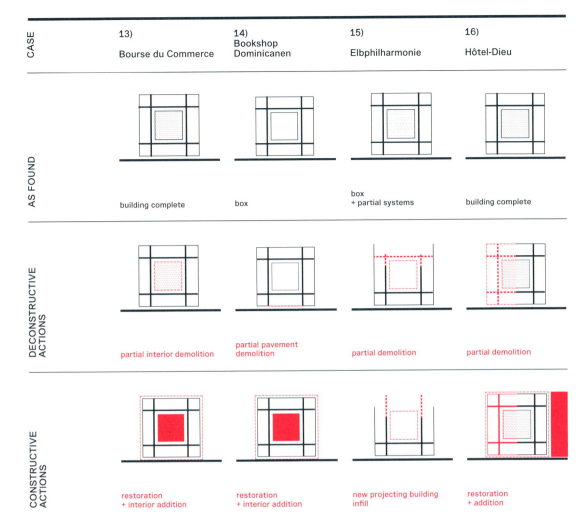

"Boxes" in terms of completeness and (de)constructive actions

This group includes four projects that intervene on buildings with a high level of preservation. Each project has adapted a built box that was potentially used without extreme interventions. However, all these pre-existing buildings were facing functional obsolescence in addition to physical deterioration. The design adaptations ensure their reuse as proper buildings with new additions, either interior or exterior. The first case, the Bourse du Commerce, is a former exchange center in the core of Paris; the second case, the Dominicanen Bookshop, is a transformed Gothic church situated in the center of Maastricht; the third case, the Elbphilharmonie in Hamburg, is an abandoned warehouse on the Elbe River; and the fourth case, the Hôtel-Dieu in Lyon, is a defunct hospital occupying an entire block.

Bourse du Commerce

Case 13

The Bourse du Commerce in Paris, located in the Les Halles district, has been transformed into the museum of the Pinault Collection, which opened in spring 2021 after three years of restoration and remodeling. The listed building has a rich historical layering, overseen by Pierre-Antoine Gautier: it includes a sixteenth-century Medici column, remains of the eighteenth-century circular grain market, Halle au Blé, and modifications from its conversion into a stock exchange, the Bourse de Commerce, in 1889.[47]

The history of the Bourse du Commerce began in 1755, when Paris acquired the land of Caterina de' Medici's palace, keeping only the Medici column. In the 1760s, architect Nicolas Le Camus de Mézières built a circular grain market, later covered by a timber dome. After a fire in 1811, the dome was replaced with a cast-iron structure by François-Joseph Bélanger. The grain market closed in 1873, and architect Henri Blondel converted it into a commodity exchange, which opened in 1889, preserving the circular portico and double-helix stairway while adding a glass-covered metal dome. (Bethenod and Robinne 2021) The demolition works of Les Halles in 1971 left a large space where the street pattern converges today, allowing the building its current prominence. (Picon 2021)

A key aspect of the Bourse du Commerce renovation was ensuring the reversibility of the intervention.[48] The original structure was constructed with metal grinders, curved brick walls, and straight iron slag walls. Its cast-iron frame, ordered from Le Creusot, weighed several tons, with an overall project cost of around 700,000 francs. (Brunet 1809)

Location	Paris, France
Function (old/new)	Grain market / Corn exchange / Art museum
Year (old/adapted)	1776 / 1889 / 2021
Architect (original/adaptation)	Nicolas Le Camus de Mézières / Francois-Joseph Bérlager / Henri Blondel / Tadao Ando Architect & Associates, Niney & Marca Architectes, Agence Pierre-Antoine Gatier
Property (old/new)	Chambre de Commerce et d'Industrie de Paris / City of Paris
Morpho-structural type (existing/addition)	Masonry + Dome / High / XXL
GSA (old/new)	10,500 m² / 10,500 m²
Height (old/new)	34 m / 9 m
Promoter (new)	Pinault Foundation
Cost[46] (old/new)	N/A / $ 120 M
Decay stage	Complete building
Basic materials (old/new)	Limestone, brick, iron / Concrete, steel
Embodied energy (retroactive/new)	72,800,602 MJ (6,933 MJ/m²) / 1,145,453 MJ (1,833 MJ/m²)

Bourse du Commerce, dimensional and morphological analysis

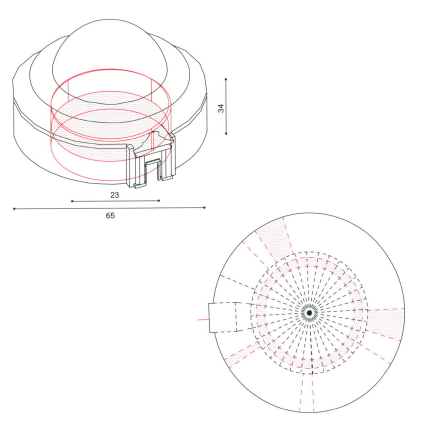

The transformation into the Pinault Collection Museum of Contemporary Art began in 2017, with François Pinault commissioning Tadao Ando to designed the 13,000-square-meter circular space,[49] along with Lucie Niney and Thibault Marca from studio NeM, who were responsible for the internal demolition and execution of Ando's cylinder design, and Pierre-Antoine Gatier with Setec Bâtiment for the restoration works. (Commission de vieux Paris 2017, 4–7)

The adaptive reuse project is a key part of a larger restoration, centered around a concrete cylinder, 9 meters high and 29 meters in diameter, with a 125-meter-long wall and a 91-meter walkable corridor. The cylinder was constructed by piercing the rotunda's floor with steel supports, allowing the concrete to be suspended from a metal frame. This method avoided the need for demolition, preserving the original structure. The hollow design of the cylinder made it possible to integrate essential systems. The curved wall, inspired by Japanese tatami mats, features 863 perforated panels and four openings. A concrete staircase leads to four exhibition levels, offering varied views of the historical building. The museum spans 13,000 square meters, with 7,700 square meters dedicated to exhibitions, including seven distinct areas, a 288-seat auditorium, a restaurant, and other services, creating a dynamic visitor experience. (Pinault Foundation 2021)

Before the restoration and adaptive reuse, the building was structurally solid and safe, despite its outdated systems.[50]

The original building's morphology is centered in both plan and section. The new design enhances these features by reinforcing the rotunda and promoting centripetal movement through the addition of a cylindrical object. A double corridor—one on the ground floor and another wrapping around the cylinder—strengthens this centralized form. Three major stairwells are strategically placed around the perimeter, serving as wedges that complement the central colonnade.

In terms of construction technology, the new cylinder is made of poured self-compacting concrete, which does not require vibration. Approximately 190 cubic meters of concrete were used for the cylinder, with 240 square meters of formwork consisting of 12 elements. The steel frame weighs around 23 tons, with a volume of almost 3 cubic meters.

The original building consists of about 11,000 cubic meters of limestone blocks and an additional 1,300 cubic meters of bricks from Blondel's refurbishment. Additionally, Blondel's iron dome weighs approximately 220 tons. (Brunet 1809) The original structure embeds more than 70,000,000 megajoules, while the new cylinder accounts for over 1,000,000 megajoules.

Bourse du Commerce – Pinault Foundation, Tadao Ando's cylinder viewed from the top, July 2021, Paris

Bookshop Dominicanen

Case 14

The Selexyz Bookstore Dominicanen is located in the heart of Maastricht, just 300 meters from the city hall. Originally a Gothic church, it was consecrated in 1294 by the Dominican Order. In 1794, during Napoleon's occupation, the church was confiscated for military use. It had been the convent church of the Maastricht Dominican Order before being repurposed as the city's depot in 1805.

This transformation significantly altered the building. The choir stalls and organ were moved to Saint Servatius Church, while pavement tiles were removed, and a partition wall and new floor were added, which severely damaged a valuable Tomas Aquinas wall painting. The city depot remained in the church until 1899, when it was relocated to the former meat market on Grote Straat. (Hovens et al. 2006, 123–56)

Thereafter, the church was used as an exhibition space, although repairs had to be postponed for at least two years due to a lack of government funding. Nonetheless, considerable work had to be done before the chapel could serve as an exhibition space. The partition wall and floor, which had been installed during its use as a depot, were demolished. A layer of grit was applied to the rough flooring as a temporary covering. (ibid., 62)

The building was first restored by architect Sprenger in 1912. In the 1960s, the convent was dismantled, making way for a department store. Shortly after the restoration, the Maastrichts Stedelijk Orkest used the church, which had undergone modifications including the installation of wooden flooring, electrical lighting, a heating system, a cloak room, and two dressing rooms. The church also served as an exhibition and celebration hall until the city archive and library moved into the chapel in the late 1960s, followed by the post office.

Since the 1980s, the space has housed a variety of uses, most recently a bicycle storage facility before its renovation. In 2006, BGN transformed the chapel into a bookstore as part of revitalizing the Entre-Deux shopping district, which replaced the former convent. The Dominican church, owned by the City of Maastricht, became part of the Entre-Deux master plan in 2000. SATIJNplus was later brought in to redesign and restore the church as part of the 2006 redevelopment project, led by Boekhandels Groep Nederland Group (BGN).[51]

Location	Maastricht, The Netherlands
Function (old/new)	Church / Bike storage / Events venue / Bookshop, cultural venue
Year (old/adapted)	1294 / 2005 / 2007
Architect (original/adaptation)	N/A / SATIJN + Architecten / Merkx+Girod Architecten
Property (old/new)	Municipality of Maastricht
Morpho-structural type (existing/addition)	Masonry structure / Frame / Medium / L
GSA (old/new)	1,480 m² / 2,362 m²
Height (old/new)	11m / 11 m
Promoter (new)	Boekhandels Groep Nederland (BGN)
Cost (old/new)	N/A / Not disclosed
Decay stage	Box
Basic materials (old/new)	Millstone grit, marble / Steel
Embodied energy (retroactive/new)	27,539,400 MJ (18,608 MJ/m²) / 3,753,313 MJ (4,255 MJ/m²)

Bookshop Dominicanen, dimensional and morphological analysis

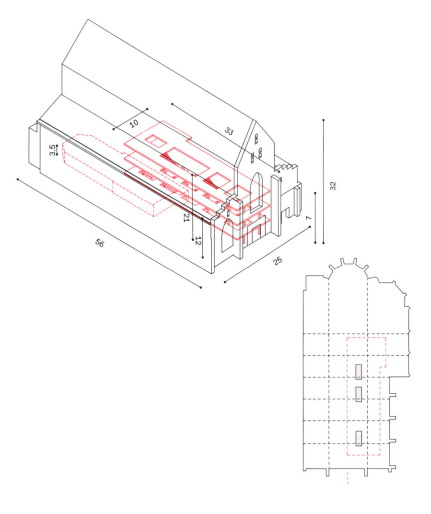

Boxes 127

The church required restoration and preparation for use, including the installation of basic electrical and heating systems. The Amsterdam-based firm Merkx+Girod Architecten designed the retail space for the Selexyz Boekhandel group, highlighting the stunning Gothic architecture with its towering heights and vaulted ceilings.

The project features a tripartite longitudinal plan, comprising a central nave that leads to a semicircular chorus and two equal side aisles. The interior spans 1,260 square meters, with the side aisles reaching about 11 meters high and the central nave rising to 20 meters. New rectangular galleries fit the aisle dimensions, with three linear staircases and an elevator providing access along the platforms.

While the church's structure and exterior were well-preserved, its internal systems were damaged. The adaptation project built on previous restoration efforts, seamlessly integrating new elements into the historical building. SATIJNplus Architecten collaborated with Merkx+Girod to design new structures as "loose elements," ensuring the preservation of the church's restored frescoes and vault paintings.

The adaptive reuse project added a four-story black steel structure, expanding the commercial space to 1,200 square meters while maintaining an open view of the interior. The design includes two upper levels to maximize space, with a bookcase in the southern aisle and low tables arranged in the northern aisle.[52] A basement was excavated beneath the original floor to accommodate restrooms and storage, and a café area was added in the chorus, featuring tables and seating that follow its curved design. Staircases and an elevator connect all four levels, providing unique views of the Gothic vaults.

In 2010, a new west portal was designed and completed with the Heritage Commission's approval, blending modern elements with historical significance while keeping the new structures independent and removable from the original marble construction.

The church features 3,700 cubic meters of original marble blocks on 340 cubic meters of millstone-grit foundations, supported by 22 steel pillars that support three platforms, adding about 850 square meters of space and 17 cubic meters of steel.

The original structure holds approximately 27,000,000 megajoules of embodied energy—relatively high for a building with a floor area under 1,500 square meters—while Merkx+Girod's addition contributes around 4,000,000 megajoules over just under 900 square meters.[53]

Bookshop Dominicanen, designed by Merkx+Girod Architecten, view from the left aisle, July 2021, Maastricht

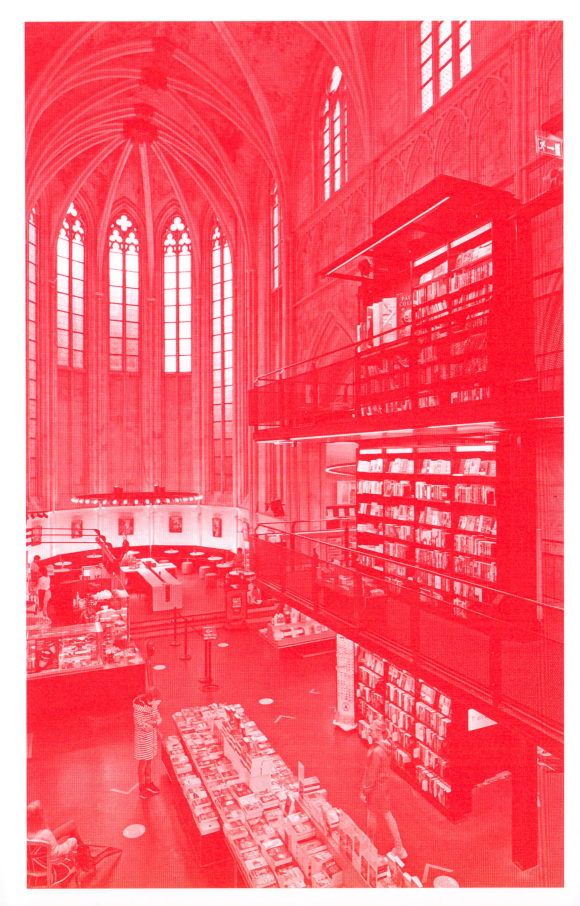

Elbphilharmonie

Case 15

The Elbphilharmonie is located in the historical Sandtorhafen district along the Elbe River, just 1.6 miles from Hamburg's city center. The original structure, Kaispeicher A, was designed by architect Werner Kallmorgen and completed in 1966, serving as a coffee warehouse until its closure in the 1990s. Elbphilharmonie Hamburg Bau GmbH & Co. KG, represented by ReGe Hamburg ProjektRealisierungsgesellschaft mbH, commissioned Herzog & de Meuron to design the new philharmonic hall. Opened in January 2017, the Elbphilharmonie includes a philharmonic auditorium, a chamber music hall, bars, restaurants, luxury apartments, a five-star hotel, a fitness center, conference spaces, a plaza, and a roof terrace affording panoramic views. The site spans 10,000 square meters, with almost 6,000 dedicated to the building and a gross floor area of about 125,000 square meters, reaching a maximum height of 110 meters. The former building has been entirely gutted, retaining only the exterior brick walls to preserve its historical appearance and house a 520-unit parking garage.
The grid of holes, measuring approximately 50 by 75 centimeters, adds a structure to the façade, rather than serving as actual windows.

Rising above the gutted Kaispeicher A, the Elbphilharmonie has a total of 17 floors—nine fewer than the original structure. The installation of the unique glass façade began on the ninth floor, which is the first level above the foundation walls, and on the Plaza.

An 82-meter-long, arched escalator starts at the main entrance, cutting diagonally through the original building, while a second escalator leads up to the Plaza, where the entrances to the concert halls are located. The project sparked a debate both about its cost and construction time. The Elbphilharmonie came at a cost of about 865 million euros instead of the originally budgeted 351,8 million, and it was completed in 2017, and not in 2010 as initially planned. (Kostka and Fiedler 2016, 34–85) Construction stopped for 11 months, requiring a long negotiation process when decision-makers arrived at a complete turnaround of the project.[55]

Location	Hamburg, Germany
Function (old/new)	Warehouse / Opera house
Year (old/adapted)	1966 / 2017
Architect (original/adaptation)	Werner Kallmorgen / Herzog & de Meuron
Property (old/new)	Alexander Gérard / City of Hamburg
Morpho-structural type (existing/addition)	Masonry – Frame – Spatial Truss / High-rise / XXL
GSA (old/new)	5,745 m² / 120,000 m²
Height[54] (old/new)	28 m / 110 m
Promoter (new)	ReGe Hamburg ProjektRealisierungsgesellschaft mbH
Cost (old/new)	Not disclosed / € 865 M
Decay stage	Box + partial systems
Basic materials (old/new)	Brick / Steel + concrete
Embodied energy (retroactive/new)	108,124,800 MJ (2,414 MJ/m²) / -72,401,280 MJ (1,616 MJ/m²) / 672,136,920 MJ (5,601 MJ/m²)

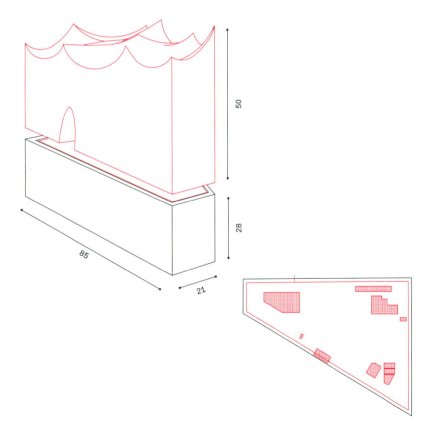

Elbphilharmonie, dimensional and morphological analysis

Boxes 131

Despite the radical approach to the pre-existing structure, Kaispeicher A was a well-maintained building, load-bearing and solid. Moreover, the existing, regular square grid, consisting of square pillars articulating eight floors, was later demolished, leaving only the foundation piles and façade standing. The additional pillars and piles serve to support the large new structures that have been added. In terms of morphology, the existing box was gutted by placing a new building inside the old one that rises above it. The original grid in the existing box organizes the service areas, parking, and technical rooms, while the 82-meter-long arched escalator climbs up through the former warehouse from the building's entrance on the east side. (Mack 2018) The journey through the illuminated tunnel-like tube leads to a panoramic window with views of the port and Landungsbrücken, while a second 20-meter-long escalator provides access to the Plaza.

The centerpiece of the new building is the Grand Concert Hall, an irregularly terraced space beneath a striking glass structure, seating 2,100 people within a 30-meter radius of the conductor.

While the scale of the new additions may challenge the relationship between the old and new elements, the design clearly distinguishes them as cohesive parts, enhanced by the elevated plaza that visually separates them. In terms of material variation, the adaptive reuse project preserved about 32 percent of existing materials, demolished 86 percent, and added almost twice the amount (193 percent).

The 10-year construction project utilized a substantial amount of materials, including 1,100 high-performance glass panels, iron frame supports, and 650 steel-reinforced concrete piles.

The preserved portion of the old building contains approximately 2,500 cubic meters of bricks and 13,090 cubic meters of concrete, accounting for about 108,000,000 megajoules of embodied energy. The gutting and demolition involved around 10,000 cubic meters of reinforced concrete, resulting in a loss of about 70,000,000 megajoules. The structural materials alone comprised roughly 63,000 cubic meters of concrete and 2,310 cubic meters of steel, contributing to nearly 700,000,000 megajoules of embodied energy.

Elbphilharmonie, designed by Herzog & de Meuron, view from the opposite quay, July 2021, Hamburg

Hôtel-Dieu

Case 16

Originally built as a hospital in 1184 by the Pontifex brothers along the banks of the Rhône, the Hôtel-Dieu underwent significant expansions in 1493 and continued to evolve through the designs of notable architects such as Jean and Ferdinand Delamonce, Antoine Picquet, César Laure, Jacques-Germain Soufflot, Paul Pascalon, and Jean-Gabriel Mortamet. The hospital operated until 2010, when it was listed for preservation as a historical monument in France. (Cayuela and Sarger 2016) After a five-year vacancy, a transformation project commenced in 2015, when Crédit Agricole Assurances acquired the Grand Hôtel Dieu, partnering with Caisse régionale de Crédit Agricole Centre-Est. Scaprim Property Management began commercialization in March 2016, leading to the opening of the Grand Hôtel-Dieu in April 2018, followed by the InterContinental Lyon Hôtel-Dieu in June 2019. The extensive restoration, overseen by architect Didier Repellin, who specializes in historical monuments, included three new buildings and a large roof structure designed by Albert Constantin and Claire Bertrand of AIA Architects, marking it as the largest adaptive reuse project in France.

The new Hôtel-Dieu spans 2.2 hectares and features 8,000 square meters of integrated courtyards and gardens. Overall, the project encompasses approximately 51,500 square meters, with 40,000 square meters of rehabilitated buildings and 11,500 square meters of new construction. The total area of intervention measures 52,000 square meters, including 40,000 square meters of façade work, 15,000 square meters of roofing, and 1,400 square meters of windows.

The project involved demolishing around 22,000 tons of materials, all meticulously sorted and removed, requiring over 2 million working hours. The new space accommodates a vibrant mix of functions: 17,100 square meters for businesses, shops, and restaurants; a five-star hotel with 138 rooms spanning 13,500 square meters; office spaces totaling 13,600 square meters, with 6,600 square meters newly constructed and 7,000 square meters adapted from existing structures; a 2,900-square-meter convention center; a "City of Gastronomy" covering 3,600 square meters; and 11 housing units totaling 800 square meters. The expansive courtyards and gardens, once parking lots, are now open to the public, fostering community engagement and enjoyment.[58]

Location	Lyon, France
Function (old/new)	Hospital / Mixed used, hotel, food court, shopping mall
Year (old/adapted)	1184 / 1493 / 2010
Architect (original/adaptation)	Jean and Ferdinand Delamonce, Antoine Picquet, César Laure, Jacques-Germain Soufflot, Paul Pascalon, and Jean-Gabriel Mortamet / Albert Constantin and Claire Bertrand (AIA Life Designers) + Didier Repellin (RL&A)
Property (old/new)	Banks of the Rhône / Crédit Agricole Assurances + Caisse régionale de Crédit Agricole Centre-Est
Morpho-structural type (existing/addition)	Masonry structure / Dome / Frame / Positive curvature shell / Negative curvature shells / Super high / XXL
GSA (old/new)	40,000 m² / + 11,500 m²
Height[56] (old/new)	24 m / 24 m
Promoter (new)	Scaprim Property Management
Cost[57] (old/new)	N/A / € 150 M
Decay stage	Complete building
Basic materials (old/new)	Stone / Steel
Embodied energy (retroactive/new)	313,593,000 MJ (7,840 MJ/m²) / -10,357,200 MJ (259 MJ/m²) / 49,166,208 MJ (4,275 MJ/m²)

Hôtel-Dieu, dimensional and morphological analysis

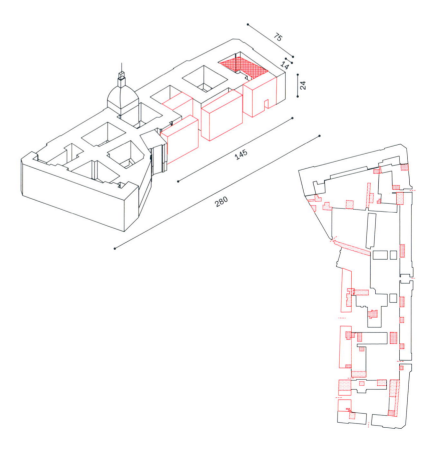

Boxes   135

The new Hôtel-Dieu project introduces three buildings that enhance the existing block's geometry and compensate for previous demolitions. The design features a commercial ground-floor base, with double-height first and second floors, and an upper level dedicated to workspaces. New façades, composed of a mix of solid and glazed sections, create a visual contrast with the historical structures. These façades use glass walls with sliding interior panels while retaining a rigid frame. The horizontal blades reflect the hollow joints used by architects Soufflot and Pascalon in their original stone designs. The project has received several awards.

The new Canopée is a glass roof over the south courtyard that spans 1,050 square meters and consists of 306 laminated glass panels, each between 2 and 8 millimeters thick and varying from 1 to 4.6 square meters. Supported by six circular metal poles—50 centimeters in diameter and averaging 14.5 meters in height—, the canopy weighs around 300 tons, of which 42 tons are glass and 260 tons are steel. The large glass elements, measuring 3.5 meters on each side, enhance visibility of the existing façade. Prefabricated and preassembled in a workshop, the canopy was welded on site.

To accommodate the varied heights of surrounding façades, architects designed a diagonally spaced mesh that avoids supports on the cornices. The original structure comprised about 55,000 cubic meters of limestone blocks, while the new buildings and canopy used approximately 210 cubic meters of steel and 34 cubic meters of structural glass. In terms of material preservation, the project retained 96 percent of the historical buildings, demolished 4 percent, and added 1 percent. The existing construction features an articulated block that opens into expansive inner courtyards. This adaptive reuse project enhances access to these courtyards and reinforces the perimeter with new buildings matching the existing height.

Overall, the project involved removing 22,000 tons of demolition waste. New additions include 40,000 square meters of double-skin façade, 15,000 square meters of roofing, 1,400 windows, and a steel and glass canopy weighing about 170 tons. The embodied energy related to structural materials is significant: the new buildings contain nearly 50,000,000 megajoules, while the existing block embed more than 300,000,000 megajoules, not accounting for the demolition, which involved materials embodying over 10,000,000 megajoules.

Hôtel-Dieu, designed by AIA Life Designers, view from the main street, July 2021, Lyon

Endnotes

1. The data is based on the construction timelines of the surrounding buildings.
2. The transformation of the parking lot into a local sports facility required a transfer of ownership from the Region to the City of Paris. Since 2007, the Duperré site has been managed by the Directorate of Youth and Sports, with its upkeep and renovation handled by the 9th arrondissement through allocated funding. (Pontecaille 2020)
3. EDF is a French multinational electric utility company, largely owned by the French state.
4. Based on the France Cadastre record (Section: AD, Sheet: 000AD01, Parcel: AD115). Requested online on 07/09/2021.
5. The Lycée Edgar Quinet is a historical institution, in particular the building at rue Duperré 24, which opened in 1864 as an Élisa Lemonnier school of applied arts for girls. Source: https://www.ac-paris.fr/serail/jcms/s2_833406/fr/l-etablissement-dans-l-histoire
6. Since the original redesign of this court, subsequent transformations of other courts have followed. The successful collaboration between Nike and Pigalle has since expanded with new courts in Beijing and Mexico City. Additionally, the court's positive influence on the neighborhood has inspired similar projects, such as the Playground Porte de Vanves, which opened in 2019 in the XIV arrondissement. (Pacciardi 2019)
7. The Can Tacó adaptive reuse project cost approximately 130,000 euros, averaging 50 euros per square meter. However, when accounting for archaeological interventions and additional facilities developed around the site, the total project cost exceeds one million euros. Funding was provided by the European Regional Development Fund (ERDF) and a nominal grant from the Ministry of Culture, with some other contributions from the company Henkel Ibérica de Montornès. (Gironés 2021)
8. In 2008, the site was listed as a "Cultural Heritage Site of National Interest (BCIN)." In 2009, the town councils initiated a project, which officially began the following year.
9. The archaeological park now features an information center, an archaeology and nature classroom, and a central esplanade with a small amphitheater. This analysis centers on the key intervention involved in adapting the ancient remains at the site.
10. Toni Girones interviewed by the author in July 2021, Barcelona.
11. Among the best-preserved features are two cisterns. The main cistern, located at the lowest level, measures approximately 10 by 4 meters, while the second cistern, positioned centrally, has a distinct L-shaped design. The main cistern was once protected from the weather by a canopy.
12. Information is based on a written release by Un Parell d'Arquitectes (Eduard Callís, Guillem Moliner) and an interview and visit on site with architect Eduard Callís in July 2021.
13. The budget does not cover the lighting system or the decorative tile work.
14. Sadurni Brunet (1886-1958) was a decorator working in the neighborhood, who specialized in designing sceneries.
15. In particular, the employed funds were part of the "Structural Funds of the Interregional Operational Program for Cultural, Natural, and Tourism Attractors" / Fondi Strutturali del Programma Operativo Interregionale. Attrattori culturali, naturali e turismo - P.O.In. 2007-2013.
16. In collaboration with Soprintendenza Beni Archeologici Regione Puglia and Segretaiato Regionale MiBACT per la Puglia.
17. Mibact's visitor data 2020. Available at https://www.ansa.it/puglia/notizie/2020/01/30/musei-mibact-40-visite-in-puglia_b516543a-fd3a-4e9c-9f7a-77f576660d9c.html. Accessed on 09/09/2021.
18. Edoardo Tresoldi, press release to the author, 25/03/2020.
19. The project was awarded the Dutch Steel Prize 2008, the Glass Award 2008, the ULI (Urban Land Institute) Global Award for Excellence 2008, the MIPIM Green Building Award and Special Jury Award 2008, and was nominated for the Mies van der Rohe Award in 2009.
20. Data and information are based on the Planning Application Form to Camden Municipality. Available at http://camdocs.camden.gov.uk/HPRM-WebDrawer/PlanRec?q=recContainer:2014/6386/P. Accessed in April 2021. Additional information was provided to the author by WilkinsonEyre Architects between July 2020 and January 2021.
21. For more details see the Grade II Listed Buildings, reference number 798-1-58891, in Camden Borough Council historical records dated October 1, 1986.
22. The development includes the ex-Granary House, now Central St Martins, the Bagley's Warehouse development by Heatherwick Studio, and the new Google HQ by BIG.
23. In 2005, the Gasholder No. 8 was restored by Shepley as well and re-erected to the west of the Gasholder Triplet site, becoming the "Gasholder Park" designed by Phillips Bell Architects.
24. The project has received multiple international design awards: Civic Trust Awards Regional; Sunday Times British Home Award; Development of the Year Award; RIBA National Award 2018; RIBA London Award 2018; International Property Awards 2016; Best International Architecture Multiple Residence, and World's Best Architecture.

25	The gasholders have volumes of roughly 229, 223, and 165 cubic meters, respectively.
26	The winning group, selected from among seven proposals, was formed by Servizi Tecnologie Sistemi S.p.A., Latz+Partner, Studio Cappato, Gerd Pfarrè, Ugo Marano, and Studio Pession Associate.
27	Taking into account the two sheds (A+B) of about 12,640 and 23,520 square meters.
28	This value relates to the crest of the pillars. The medium height is estimated at 24 meters.
29	The shed still visible is the former "stripping" building, referring to the action of extracting steel ingots from the mold in which they are produced, carried out by hydraulic pistons hitting the ingot mold.
30	See official soil pollution report, Comune di Torino, Monitoraggi Ambientali Spina 3, 2012-2021. Available at http://www.comune.torino.it/ambiente/news/monitoraggi-ambientali-spina-3.shtml. The "Comitato Dora Spina 3" commented on the data. Available at http://www.comitatodoraspina3.it/bonifiche. Accessed on 10/10/2021.
31	In terms of energy variation, it is not correct to talk about "energy loss," and the demolished material would not be included in LCA-based evaluation. Here, the term "lost energy" is used to indicate the impact of demolition on the energy embedded in the existing materials. However, dismantled materials are not included in the embodied energy calculation of the LCA.
32	On January 16, 2024, the Municipality of Lisbon (CML) addressed the Panorâmico de Monsanto in the "102nd Plenary Meeting of the Lisbon Municipal Assembly (AML) for the 2021-2025 term, 67th Extraordinary Session." The meeting's record is available online at https://www.youtube.com/watch?v=S3krUW0fOzQ. Furthermore, on January 19, 2024, *The Portugal News* published an article titled "Lisbon Landmark to Undergo Facelift," detailing that the building, which once operated as a restaurant and reopened to the public as a viewpoint in 2017, is now under study for restoration. This article is available at https://www.theportugalnews.com/news/2024-01-19/lisbon-landmark-to-undergo-facelift/85239. Accessed on 07/10/2024.
33	Costs are confirmed both by an architect's release and news. (Oliveres i Guixer 2018; LIN Architects 2007; Séron-Pierre 2007)
34	Originally designed by Albert Speer and built on the site of the old transatlantic port, the Saint-Nazaire submarine base was constructed in about a year and a half using forced labor during the German occupation. Its controversial history has made it a contested piece of heritage for half a century, with demolition seen as the preferred option after World War II.
35	By 1998, the city had purchased the base and removed the rear parts of several wings, paving the way for its current use.
36	The roof accommodates the radome, a geodesic dome originally used to cover radar at Berlin's Tempelhof Airport. Made of an aluminum frame with nearly 300 triangular sections, the dome is covered with a translucent membrane.
37	As confirmed by the fieldwork in July 2021, the project "B.À.SE" won a competition to turn the base's roof into an open-air display of technical and agricultural solutions. Its completion has been delayed due to the pandemic.
38	RTS and C & E Engineering were the structural consultants, and Michel Desvigne was the landscape consultant. EIFFAGE was the general contractor.
39	In detail, SEMAPA is the developer of the project, funded by Caisse des Depots for the client SCI Docks en Seine.
40	According to the interview with Ábel Zsendovits, manager of Szimpla Kert, the property is managed by a new private owner. His name has not been disclosed despite several attempts during the interview.
41	Relating to the height of the main façade
42	Record Budapest Buildings Archive. Accessed on 22/07/2021 at Budapest Föváros Levéltára.
43	The documentary materials at the "Budapest Föváros Levéltára," at Teve utca 3-5, in Budapest, along with the support of Telek Ágnes, team leader of the planning and mapping section, have enabled a retracing of the building's evolution. While no recent plans are available, the oldest dates back to 1891, and the latest is from 1961. The drawings are based on on-site visits and use the 1961 plan as a foundation
44	Interview with Szimpla Kert's manager, Ábel Zsendovits, on July 23, 2021 in Budapest.
45	In 2019, the psychiatric center's safety committee determined that the risk of accidents for patients was too high and decided to close the stairs. (Boie 2019) Safety concerns also arose regarding the roof, necessitating repairs on the first level. During a site visit in July 2021, the author observed that the facility had been closed for three months for repair work.
46	The only data available is about the original building, which cost about 700,000 francs in 1809.
47	According to the land registry (cad. 01; 02 AS 60) and the *Classé MH partiellement, inscrit MH partiellement, protection totale*, the building is listed as French heritage since January 15, 1975, in particular, the stock exchange, excluding the classified part; registration by decree of January 15, 1975; the dome with its décor classification by decree of June 20, 1986.

48	According to NeM architects, Tadao Ando's cylindrical structure could be removed without damaging the original building. (Pinault Foundation 2021, 19)
49	Tadao Ando has a long-standing working relationship with Pinault. In particular, he designed the conversion projects for Palazzo Grassi and Punta della Dogana in Venice.
50	Pierre-Antoine Gatier highlighted the importance of restoring the building to its 1889 status, considered the most advanced of its time, focusing on the dome and the frescos, with the dome being the most challenging feature to preserve. To tackle this, TESS engineering were brought in to reinforce the cast-iron framework while maintaining its authenticity.
51	The restoration also included 1,400 square meters of frescoes, overseen by curator Alix Laveau from the Direction des Musées de France. This work aimed to remediate past alterations and the effects of aging, as the frescoes had accumulated dirt, mold had altered their colors, and the pictorial layer had suffered degradation in many areas.
52	Private correspondence with SatijnPlus Architects (Rob Brouwers, in charge of the project)
53	The placement on the south aisle was to protect a significant fresco of Thomas Aquinas on the north side.
54	In 2018, a new structure was added to the northern aisle to house CD-ROMs and DVDs. This second addition, half the length and height of the first, was created in collaboration with Maastricht's technical office and at the request of Boekhandel Dominicanen. Considered more furniture than architecture, this prefabricated, lightweight structure is not intended to be permanent. Despite the on-site research and a correspondence with Ton Harmes, the director of Boekhandel Dominicanen, it was not possible to access the technical drawings at the Maastricht's archive. Therefore, no specific technical data are currently available. However, according to the survey, this structure is considered a temporary furniture.
55	Considering the maximum height
56	The height considered is the medium height of the block according to the architectural drawing of AIA Life Designers.
57	According to RL&A, VAT excluded and including all the restoration procedures
58	This analysis excludes restoration works, as it requires a detailed examination. It focuses on the additions and their relationship with the existing block.
59	Grand Jury Special Prize Trophées du Cadre de Vie – 2018 Fimbacte Festival; Regional Grand Prize 2017 Pyramides d'argent; Golden Trophy "Best real estate operation" SIATI 2016; Jury's Prize at the 2018 SIMI Grand Prize. Source: AIA Architects.

COMPARATIVE TABLES:

TIME OPPORTUNITIES, SPATIAL PATTERNS, AND ENERGY DYNAMICS OF FORM

An ideal type is formed by the one-sided accentuation of one or more points of view and by the synthesis of a great many diffuse, discrete, more or less present and occasionally absent concrete individual phenomena, which are arranged according to those one-sidedly emphasized viewpoints into a unified analytical construct. [...] (Weber et al. 1949, 90)

The previous chapter presented 16 case studies, alongside additional brief examples, using the proposed analytical categories: *footprints*, *shells*, *structures*, and *boxes*. These terms were initially introduced with their common meanings, but their definitions are reinterpreted based on their transformative potential, as informed by the case studies. *Footprints* refer to structures made primarily of masonry systems. If there are additions, they involve arches, domes, or frame systems with varying dimensions. Most are located outside urban areas, except Case 1 in Paris. No projects expanded the gross surface area, and due to the low starting height, no increases in height were made. *Structures* consist only of frame systems, such as spatial or portal frames, and are typically large-scale (over 2,500 square meters), with heights often exceeding 20 meters. Transformations of these projects involved structural additions or modifications that increased both height and surface area. The *shells* category includes a variety of systems, from masonry to frame structures, which are transformed solely using frame structures. Original heights of 20 to 50 meters are either maintained or slightly increased. While demolition was initially considered, various reasons led to its rejection: Case 9 was impractical to demolish, Cases 11 and 12 were already partially demolished, and Case 10 was listed for preservation. *Boxes* encompass a wide range of structural systems due to the extensive preservation of existing buildings. Sizes range from 1,500 to 40,000 square meters, with medium to tall heights. Most projects used frame systems, except for Case 13, where concrete walls were poured. Among these cases, all original buildings are heritage-protected, except for Case 15.

The following comparative tables illustrate these varying degrees of transformation, from minimal to extensive. The urban context also influenced these adaptations, revealing a mutual relationship between the building and its environment—street pattern, built pattern. The spatial asset of these buildings pictures a wide range of footprints, plans, axonometric views, sections, morphological schemes, circulation, and structural rhythms. These changes exemplify the transformation process when analyzed against time, layer removal, and addition.

Material flow—both qualitatively and quantitatively—tracks how much material is involved in adaptive reuse and the ratio of old to new. The embodied energy of these materials is key to assessing sustainability and resource preservation. These factors illustrate the non-linear relationship between existing conditions and transformations, framing the potential for change.

The projects demonstrate significant variation in form, structure, and spatial characteristics, highlighting the challenge of measuring the transformative potential of form. While not strictly quantifiable, the interplay between time, spatial elements, and material energy reflects the transformations undergone. Along with these 16 cases, the more than 50 "unexpected" cases and "examples" of adaptation collected on the route conclude this section with a wide range of form variations outlined, available on the website www.atlasofpotential.com.

Looking at architectural adaptations, the categories—*footprints*, *structures*, *shells*, and *boxes*—are redefined in terms of transformative potential, describing how existing conditions shape future design possibilities:

Footprint
Marginal traces of existing structures, such as foundations, partial walls, and delimited areas, that enable the reuse of the encompassed space through additive interventions.

Structure
Skeleton of an existing building, encompassing a range of completeness, that allows for its use as infrastructure and/or scans the integration of any new construction.

Shell
Exoskeleton of a structure that is partially or totally covered by an envelope and is suitable for hosting additions or being divided into inhabitable spaces. It acts as an open or closed container.

Box
Space enclosed by continuous walls and roofing that clearly distinguishes interior from exterior due to existing systems and requires additions, partial demolitions, or restorations to be optimally repurposed.

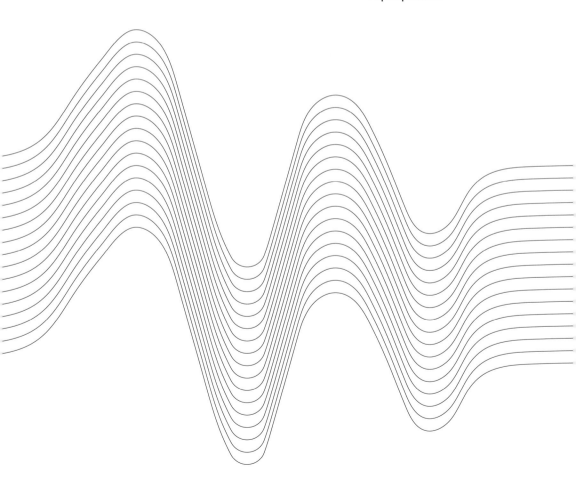

Time opportunities, spatial patterns, and energy dynamics of form

Comparative table,
photos of all cases

Comparative Tables

144

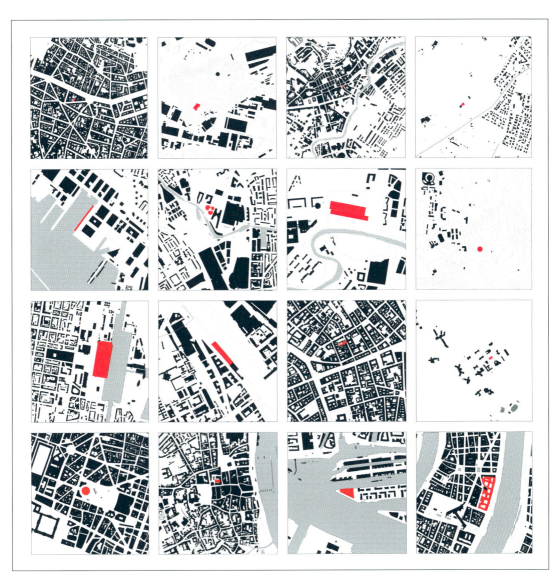

Comparative table,
built patterns

Time opportunities, spatial patterns, and energy dynamics of form

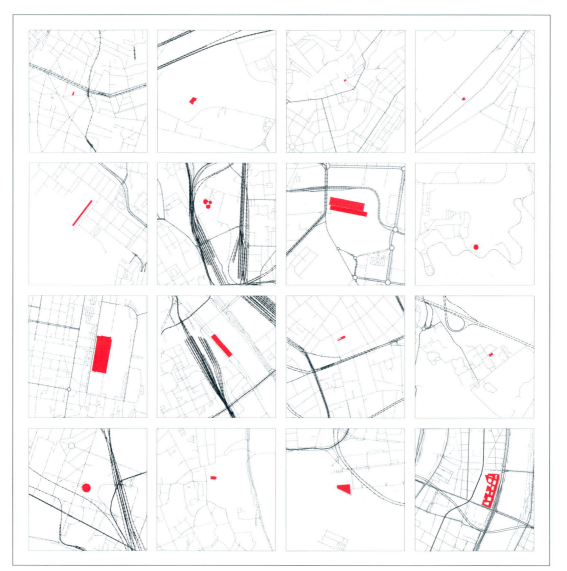

Comparative table,
street patterns

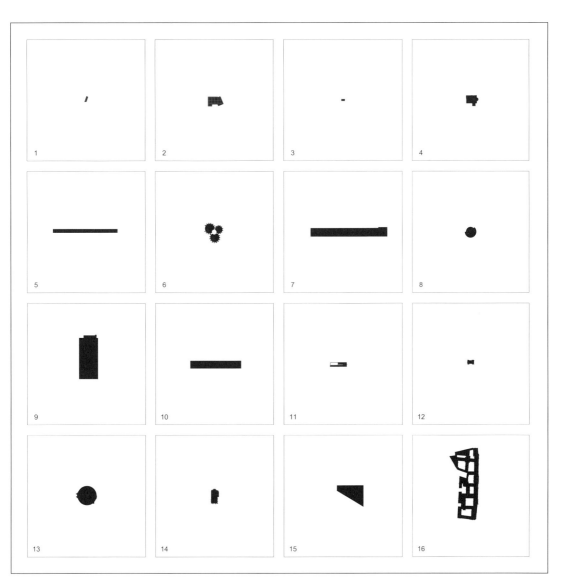

Comparative table,
footprint patterns

Time opportunities, spatial patterns, and energy dynamics of form

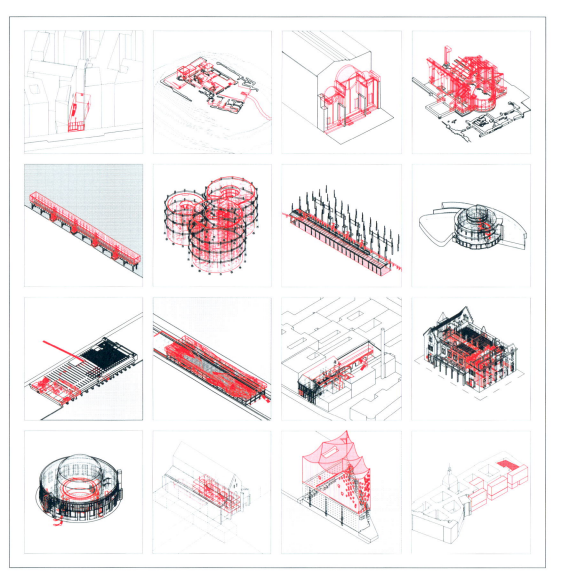

Comparative table,
axonometric views

Comparative Tables 148

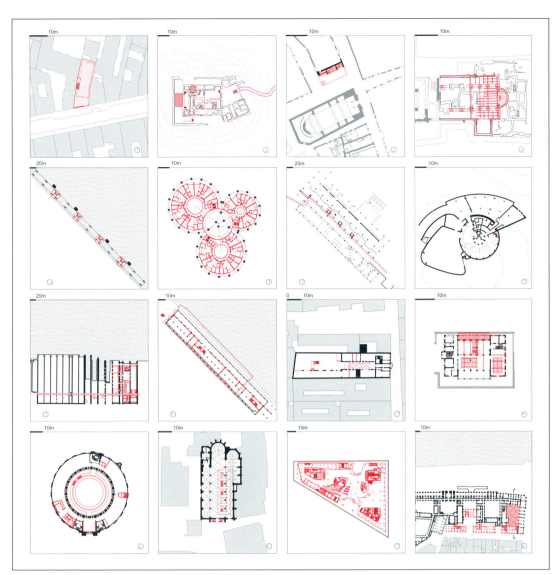

Comparative table,
plans

Time opportunities, spatial patterns, and energy dynamics of form   149

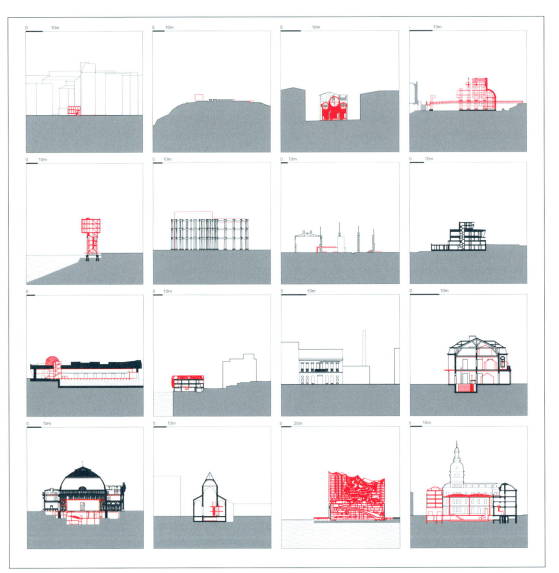

Comparative table,
sections

Comparative Tables

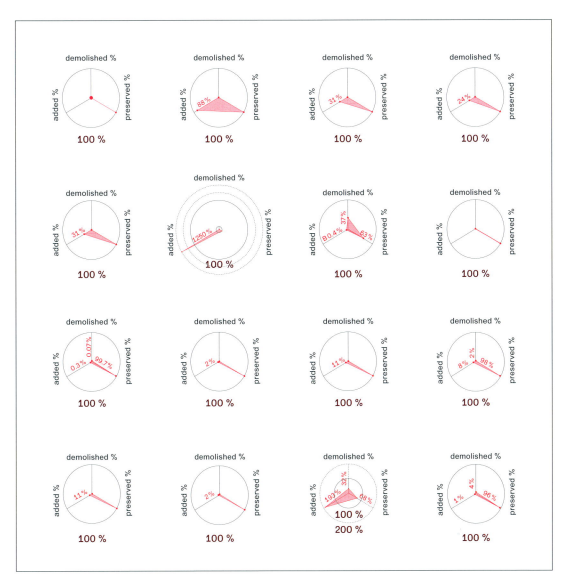

Comparative table, morphological and circulation schemes

Time opportunities, spatial patterns, and energy dynamics of form

CONCLUSIONS:
TOWARD SUSTAINABLE FORMS OF TRANSFORMATIONS

This book delves into a conceptual shift in how we define buildings in terms of potential(s), exploring a method that keeps together time, space, and materiality. The transformative potential of architectural form isn't a fixed formula or a strict definition; rather, it serves as a lens through which we can understand the underlying forces driving building adaptations. This raises essential questions: What can we uncover by analyzing buildings from multiple perspectives? How can an interdisciplinary approach help us navigate architectural complexity—not to solve it but to enable a nuanced understanding through conscious simplification?

How can data strengthen our intuitive sense that existing buildings are reservoirs of diverse forms of energy—energies embedded in construction materials and already expended in past efforts? In an era when wasting labor, energy, and natural resources is untenable, it becomes vital to harness this stored energy in ways that honor and preserve the value of what has already been created. The transformative potential is a way to look at a sustainable form of adaptation.

Paradigm shift,
thinking in terms of potential.
Scheme by the author

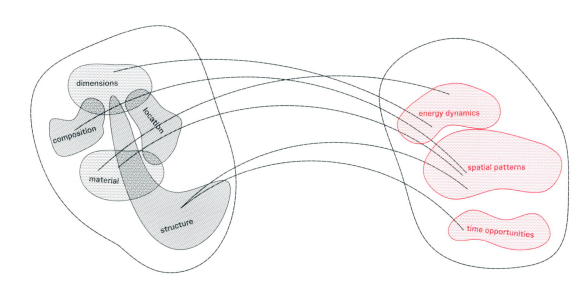

elements of form   potentials of form

Toward sustainable forms of transformations   153

Cross-readings of potential(s)

Speaking of time opportunities. During a visit to the Pinault Collection at the Bourse de Commerce in Paris, beneath its stunning glass dome, I encountered Urs Fischer's extraordinary wax rendition of "The Rape of the Sabine Women" by sixteenth-century Florentine sculptor Giambologna.[1] Each morning, wicks were placed and new holes were bored to ignite the sculpture, prompting its slow and deliberate destruction over six months. This daily transformation offered a unique experience, as the sculpture's form shifted continuously, driven by the forces of intentional decay. Here, time—a force typically resisted in art that is meant to endure—was instead embraced, underscoring its power to erode even what was crafted to last.

In architecture, a similar dynamic unfolds. Buildings, made to endure decades if not centuries, are unavoidably subject to decay. This inevitability raises essential questions about how structures age, what stages of deterioration they pass through, and the decisions made at critical junctions when their original purposes can no longer be fulfilled. It is in these moments, when decay renders a building unsuitable for its original function, that adaptive reuse becomes an option. Through intentional intervention, new life and purpose can be infused into a structure, with or without additional design alterations. In many cases, the specific forms of deterioration suggest unique adaptation pathways, providing new opportunities for imaginative reuse.

The case studies analyzed here reveal how deeply the passage of time and the marks it leaves—whether through physical decay or functional obsolescence—shape architectural approaches to transformation. The concept of "shearing layers" is particularly relevant in this context, providing a robust framework for understanding and harnessing these opportunities. This analysis points to the need for a more nuanced approach to these layers, especially regarding the core elements of a building's architectural form, such as its structural bulk.

■ 3, 12, 21, 30

To employ them as a toolkit to retrace the adaptation of form, the schematization of (de)constructive actions should be addressed in terms of layers, too. ■ It makes the process of adaptation clear and unavoidable, sheds light on the relationship between the physical completeness of a building and the adaptation possibilities, and gives some hint on what is more likely to be embraced through an architectural project.

Within specific conditions, can a conscious incompleteness be successfully embraced as a design strategy? We might say it

■ 2, 3, 4, 7, 8, 9, 11, 12

can. ■ Not all buildings should be adapted following the logic of completeness. Perhaps, when starting from scratch, not become

■ 1, 2, 3, 4

a building at all ■, embracing their incompleteness, the void itself. Perhaps, making the unfinished, the unpolished, a distinctive

■ 4, 8, 9, 11, 12
■ 8, 9   ■ 12
■ 11, 4

mark ■ for diverse reasons: waiting for the investment to come, the difficulty of getting rid of it in the first place ■, experimenting ■, gaining attention from tourists ■, or even a combination of all of them. Furthermore, some of these "incomplete" adaptations were never "complete" in the first place, because they were

■ 7, 9, 10, 14, 15
■ 5, 6

originally infrastructure ■ or built to host a specific use only as industrial, military, and religious buildings. ■

Conclusions

Shearing layers, readapted from Stewart Brand's *How Buildings Learn* (1995). Elaboration by the author

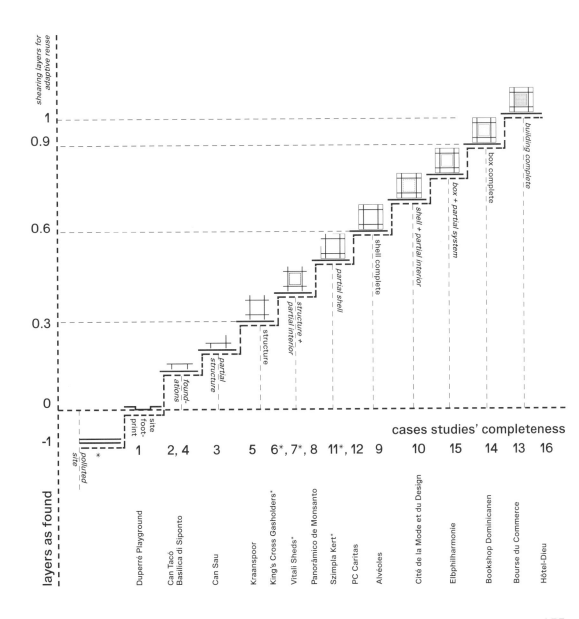

Toward sustainable forms of transformations

Page 144–51

(In)completeness is a pillar of the adaptive reuse strategies, and these layers addressed here, both in terms of "as found" and in terms of (de)constructive actions, are a toolkit to read it.

Speaking of spatial patterns. Morphological variations in spatial terms emerge from the critical redrawing of these projects, as shown in the comparative tables. ■ Can we define some deformative attitudes of the existing building that are complementary to the previous shearing layer analysis?

Indeed, by assuming spatial flexibility as a feature that affects a potential transformation of existing building forms, while cross-comparing dimensional features in terms of qualitative variations, massing, structural rhythms, and configuration of what exists before and after the last transformation of the building.

Morphological schemes are discussed by highlighting the need for expanding the intervention type analysis from a composite perspective of the form-form relationship to a configurative attitude; this can be achieved by proposing spatial types that show a tendency in the overall transformation.

Nevertheless, the types of intervention generally applied in the existing literature on the evolution of form in adaptive reuse do not include all the morphological assets evinced by the case studies. Intervention types are discussed to unravel the spatial dynamic of deformation, resulting from multiple hybridizations of multiple interventions, yet the structure is a crucial element in morphological variability. Can we define "attitudes," in the sense of predispositions inherent to the original object? To do so, a definition of the morphologies found in all the 16 case studies presented here is not enough; it is a partial reading of the complexity that structures the built environment. However, along the route of the "Atlas of Potential,"[2] the comparative reading in terms of form-form relationship helps a broader contextualization. Yet in part, the galaxy of other adaptations, both "example" (broadly recognized as adaptive reuse interventions) and "unexpected" finds (coincidentally discovered along the route of this European fieldwork) gives us a picture of such complexity.

Variations in "Examples" and "Unexpected" adaptations found along the route of case studies. July–August 2021

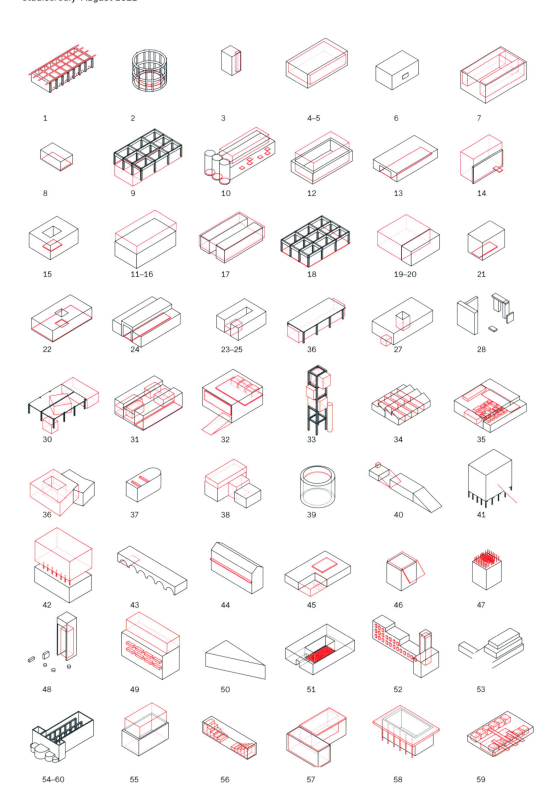

Toward sustainable forms of transformations

157

#	Additional cases	Location	Type	Actions	Existing morphology
1	Ore Bunker Gallery	Duisburg	example	envelope cut open + link + vegetation	clustered open slab
2	Gasholder Park (No. 8)	London	example	restoration + reassembly	round frame
3	Torre Arsenale	Venice	example	interior link	interior link
4	Rehearsal room	Lyon	unexpected	new interior	urban room
5	Ancienne chaufferie de l'hôpital	Lyon	example	new interior	rectangular block
6	Church Bon-Pasteur	Lyon	unexpected	closed box	rectangular box
7	Citroën garage	Lyon	example	interior remodeling + infill	tripartite block
8	Flower shop	Lyon	unexpected	interior conversion	urban room
9	H7	Lyon	example	exposure + addition of interior + plug-in	tripartite sheds + façade
10	La Sucrière	Lyon	example	vertical extension + interior + plug-in	tripartite sheds + cylinders
11	Offices AEA sub-elevation	Lyon	unexpected	vertical extension	rectangular block
12	Opéra Lyon	Lyon	example	building infill	large rectangular box
13	West Parrache Tunnel	Lyon	unexpected	opening + consolidation + surface	underground longitudinal void
14	Ancient Roman wall	Clermont-Ferrand	unexpected	building	large wall
15	Hotel Savaron	Clermont-Ferrand	unexpected	courtyard conversion	courtyard block
16	Union Régionale CFTC	Nantes	unexpected	vertical extension	rectangular block
17	École supérieure des beaux-arts	Nantes	example	skin + interior addition	longitudinal sheds
18	Le Parc des Chantiers	Nantes	example	skin removal + consolidation	tripartite large shed
19	Le Théâtre Saint-Nazaire	Saint-Nazaire	example	building extension	longitudinal block
20	Saint-Nazaire School of Fine Arts	Saint-Nazaire	unexpected	building extension	longitudinal block
21	Blockhaus, abri énergie	Saint-Nazaire	unexpected	no intervention	massive, closed box
22	Galeries Lafayette Champs-Élysées	Paris	example	conversion + interior remodeling	polymorph courtyard block
23	Rue Duhesme insertion	Paris	unexpected	filling of void	small urban enclosure
24	Le 104 Paris	Paris	example	open nave + infill	tripartite large shed
25	Rue des Cottages insertion	Paris	unexpected	filling of void	rectangular urban enclosure
26	Unnamed along the Seine	Paris	unexpected	filling of existing iron structure	filled existing frame
27	Buda Art Centre	Kotrijk	example	cutting of void + pavilion entrance	large slab
28	Ancient church	Ablain-Saint-Nazaire	unexpected	ruination	arches and walls
29	Unnamed next to a café	Kortrijk	unexpected	interior conversion	urban room
30	Hachiko Center	Bottelare	unexpected	addition + interior conversion + extension	longitudinal sheds
31	Cinema Lumière	Maastricht	example	new interior + bridge	tripartite large shed
32	Ru Paré Community	Amsterdam	example	interior boxes + horizontal division + new access + open façade	double-height block
33	Faralda NDSM Crane Hotel Amsterdam	Amsterdam	example	infill + link	vertical modular structure
34	Nieuwe Jonkerstraat Apartments	Amsterdam	unexpected	interior partition + roof cuts	longitudinal sheds
35	NDSM Loods	Amsterdam	example	interior additions	large slab
36	Utopia Library	Aalst	example	building extension	L-shaped block
37	Levi's Church	Olot	unexpected	consolidation + system	one-nave shed
38	COOP	Anderlecht	example	link + partition + vertical extension + new interior	two parallel blocks
39	Landschaftspark tank	Duisburg	example	consolidation + system addition	empty cylinder

Conclusions

40	Eichbaum	Essen	example	slight additions	tunnel
41	Ruhr Museum	Essen	example	interior partition + link	elevated box
42	Fenix I	Rotterdam	example	new interior + vertical extension	large slab
43	Hofpleinlijnviaduc	Rotterdam	unexpected	consolidation + light infill + systems	elevated track on arches
44	Telecom building	Rotterdam	example	balcony addition + interior remodeling	longitudinal block
45	The Zure Bom + Het Poolcafé	Rotterdam	unexpected	extension + light infill + systems	double sheds
46	Energiebunker	Hamburg	unexpected	new interior + systems	massive block
47	St. Pauli Bunker	Hamburg	unexpected	hat addition + vegetation	massive block
48	St. Nikolai Church	Hamburg	unexpected	link	ruinous tower
49	Jazzloft	Budapest	example	balcony addition + vertical extension	longitudinal block
50	Gólya presszó	Budapest	unexpected	roof conversion + consolidation	ruinous triangular shed
51	Élesztő	Budapest	unexpected	surface addition	courtyard block
52	Piatnik apartments	Budapest	unexpected	window extension + interior partition + link	L-shaped block
53	St. Peter's Seminary	Cardross	example	consolidation + ruination	ziggurat slab, L-shaped
54	Museu Arqueológico do Carmo,	Lisbon	unexpected	consolidation	tripartite longitudinal structure
55	Casa Altinho	Lisbon	example	new building infill	open regular box
56	Fabra I Coats social housing	Barcelona	example	new boxes infill + link	longitudinal box
57	Lleialtat Santsenca	Barcelona	unexpected	new infill + roof	L-shaped block
58	Mercat de Santa Caterina	Barcelona	example	roof addition	large shell
59	El Born Centre de Cultura i Memòria	Barcelona	example	interior addition + excavation	large shell
60	Abbazia di San Galgano	Siena	example	consolidation	tripartite longitudinal structure

Table of "examples" and
"unexpected" adaptations
defined in terms of
existing morphology and
adaptive reuse actions.

■ Page 64   Back to the 16 projects shown in Part 2 ■, the analysis of rhythms and configuration led to establishing a tendency already embedded in the existing form.

Configurative schemes
of structure and connection

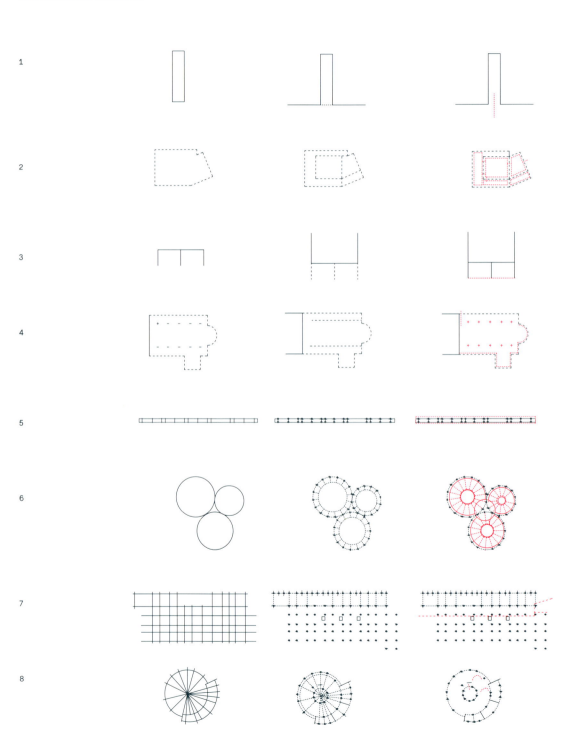

Conclusions

160

Toward sustainable forms of transformations

161

In other words, after examining transformation through (de)constructive actions, focusing on layers and deformations, these schemes establish a connection between the morphology of the existing building and its adapted state. In particular, by describing transformation in morphological terms rather than abstract intervention types, we incorporate a diachronic perspective, using concepts like shearing layers and energy flows to characterize transformation.

For "layers as found," case studies classify existing morphologies into types such as urban enclosure, spine walls, container frame, platform, and ruin shell. Each type of existing morphology is linked to a potential transformed morphology, such as an open urban box, elevated platform, panoramic exoskeleton, or infilled modular box. These transformations demonstrate how constructive and deconstructive actions are influenced by the initial morphology, rather than relying on universal intervention methods.

The diversity in transformations highlights that similar actions can produce varied results depending on the starting morphology. This variability underscores that the transformative potential of architecture relies significantly on the spatial characteristics of the original structure. For example, an urban enclosure can evolve into an open urban box with a simple surface addition, spine walls may become an urban nook, and a container frame might transform into a caged cylinder. This suggests that the classification of potential is not purely spatial but always tied to the intended outcome of the architectural project.

In conclusion, adaptive reuse offers a nuanced interplay between original and transformed forms. This approach respects and reimagines the architectural potential of existing spaces, recognizing that the transformative power of form is embedded in the unique spatial conditions of each structure.

Speaking of energy dynamics of form. The adaptive reuse projects considered have revealed a part of the transformative potential embedded in the existing layers and the morphological asset of these projects, but then it comes to considering a crucial component of the architectural form: the materials and their relative embodied energy.[3]

#	Case study	Existing morphology	Layers as found	Layers' deconstructive actions	Layers' constructive actions	Transformed morphology
1	Duperré Playground	urban enclosure	site footprint	none	surface addition	open urban box
2	Can Tacó	isolated track	building footprint	soil removal	soil addition	platform circuit
3	Cau Sau	spine walls	building wall	pavement removal	canopy addition	urban nook
4	Basilica di Siponto	foundation	building foundations	crest levelling	frame addition	ideal frame
5	Kraanspoor	platform	building structure	none	building addition + vertical links	elevated box
6	King's Cross Gasholders	container frame	building structure + partial interior	disassembly + removal of interior	soil remediation + new building + reassembled structure	caged cylinder
7	Vitali Sheds	shed frame	building structure + partial interior	partial demolition + removal of interior	surface addition + links	open canopy
8	Panorâmico de Monsanto	round slabs	building structure + partial interior	partial removal of interior	consolidation	panoramic exoskeleton
9	Alvéoles	clustered slab	building shell + interiors	cutting of envelope	interior addition + roof links	incremental stripe hub
10	Cité de la Mode et du Design	grid block	building shell + partial interior	skin demolition	interior partition + plug-over	infilled modular box
11	Szimpla Kert	ruin shell	partial building shell	none	consolidation + reassembly + ruination	active court ruin
12	PC Caritas	pavilion under demolition	partial building shell	cutting of envelope	consolidation + ruination + infill	multilayer square
13	Bourse du Commerce	rotunda	complete building	partial interior demolition	restoration + interior addition	multilevel ring
14	Bookstore Dominicanen	tripartite shed	building box	partial pavement demolition	restoration + interior addition	interior panoramic shelf
15	Elbphilharmonie	polygonal box	building box + partial systems	partial demolition	new projecting building infill	overflowing building
16	Hôtel-Dieu	polymorph courtyard block	complete building	partial demolition	restoration + addition	permeable courtyard block

■ Page 53

Assuming the transformative potential of form as a tendency inherent in its intrinsic structure and related to its matter and spatial articulation, ■ physical assets might reveal themselves as a "morphogenetic potential of matter."[4] Here, the transformative potential is also evaluated as stagnant energy stored in construction materials. Considering the matter that structures the space, we can challenge how materials could be included in a transformative perspective. In terms of potential, the material is relevant based on what "has been shaped out of the matter," more than the matter itself as an inherent mass of materials, and evaluating them in the framework of potential requires a theoretical shift from a static before-after perspective to the logic of a dynamic process.[5]

■ Page 52

Each material has a unique intensity value representing the energy required to transform it into a construction element. These intensity values are measured in MJ/kg or MJ/m^3 ■, where the embodied energy for each case varies with the flow of construction materials.

Variations in main structural materials in logarithmic scale

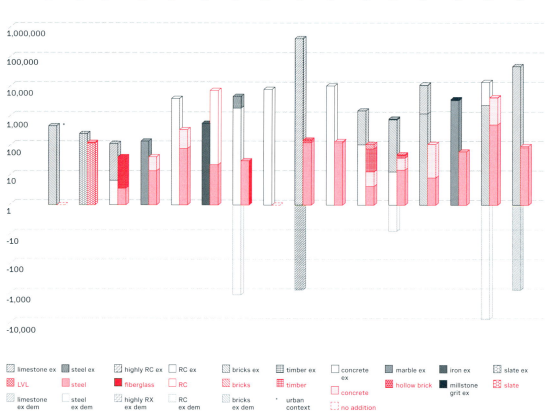

Conclusions 164

The total embodied energy, measured in megajoules (MJ), can be categorized as existing embodied energy (EEex), embodied energy from new materials (EEnew), and embodied energy from demolition materials (EEdem) ■. For interventions requiring no additional primary structural materials, there is no increase in embodied energy from Time F (when adaptive reuse began) to Time T (when the transformation phase is completed). Examples include the Duperré Playground in Paris and the Panorâmico de Monsanto in Lisbon. ■ In the former case, the perimeter walls belong to surrounding buildings, making it a zero embodied energy case. In the case of the Panorâmico, consolidation and a ruination approach preserved the reinforced concrete structure, retaining the energy embedded in these materials.

■ see figure below

■ 1, 8

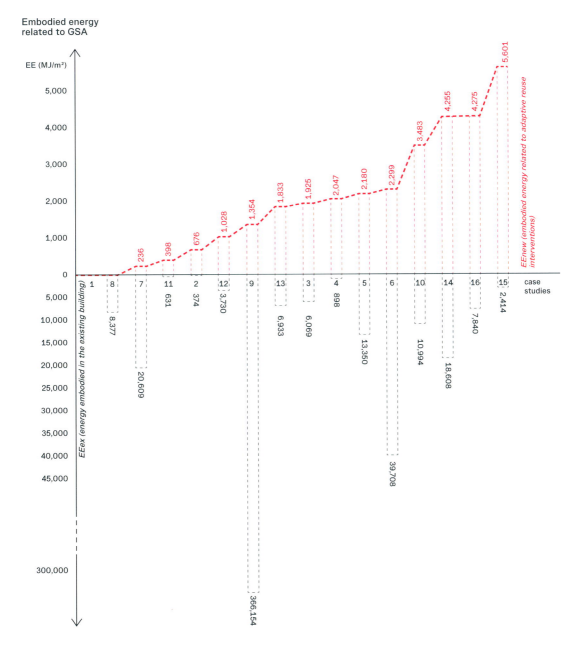

Toward sustainable forms of transformations

Some EEex values are remarkably high. For instance, the Saint-Nazaire base ■ holds over 14 billion MJ of embodied energy stuck in the highly reinforced concrete mass, and the Vitali Sheds originally contained over 1.2 billion MJ based on the structure as found in 2004. Since then, considering the steel that has been dismantled, the adaptation leaves approximately 750 million MJ of preserved existing energy.

In most cases, the energy embedded in new materials is lower than that in preserved ones. Only 3 out of 16 cases ■ show higher embodied energy from new additions than from existing materials. This balance suggests a thoughtful approach to transformation, where each intervention is assessed relative to the impact of materials already in place.

Direct comparisons can clarify embodied energy as a metric, especially by converting megajoules (MJ) to kilowatt hours (kWh) to give a tangible sense of the energy embodied in each transformation. For instance, the energy embedded in the former submarine base in Saint-Nazaire (Alvéoles) is equivalent to the energy needed for the entire city of Rome's electric energy consumption for almost 5 months.[6] The former Vitali Shed, now a skate-park and green space, if accounting for the full process, contains energy comparable to one week of Rome's electricity consumption, similar to the Elbphilharmonie's new addition. The Hôtel-Dieu's main materials equate to 3 days, and the Cité de la Mode et du Design holds 2 days worth. The Panorâmico de Monsanto, which retains its embodied energy solely in pre-existing materials, stores about 34,000 kWh—equivalent to 15 hours of electricity for Rome or the energy needed for 2,300 Tesla cars to drive 100,000 kilometers.

The Bourse de Commerce, including its new concrete cylinder, could theoretically power Rome for 20 minutes, and the Kraanspoor for almost 6 hours, considering the additions only. Even relatively low values represent significant energy: Szimpla Kert stores almost 500,000 kWh, the equivalent of powering 40 Teslas for 100,000 kilometers, and PC Caritas contains enough for over twice as many of them to travel the same distance. There is a wide range in "footprints," from 730,000 kWh for Can Tacò ■ to zero embodied energy in the Duperré Playground. For example, Can Sau holds enough energy to operate 1,000 Nintendo Switches continuously for a year, and the new Basilica di Siponto could power 33 ovens for a year.

These values underscore the importance of considering embodied energy in adaptive reuse, especially for resources-intensive structures like the Saint-Nazaire base ■. With its substantial materials and robust form, the structure presents a case for preservation rather than deconstruction, especially given its potential for incremental additions. By contrast, the zero-energy Duperré Playground ■ could accommodate various transformations, except for deconstructive actions, since there is nothing to dismantle. While theoretically recyclable materials reduce embodied energy, these examples highlight the potential of adaptive reuse to preserve resources and reduce waste.

Trajectories and clusters of potential(s)

Drawn trajectories are relatively exclusive but not univocal in absolute terms, and they show the realized tendency of existing buildings, embedding the exclusion of other potential trajectories.

We might say that the transformative potential is therefore displayed as a set of evolution trajectories of architectural forms. Such trajectories show that deconstructive approaches are applied in the majority of adaptive reuse processes. Existing buildings are partially demolished, and some elements are removed, not to be replaced but to allow the insertions of other grafts.

As in the biological evolution of forms, existing forms change under specific actions and triggers, defining new morphologies that were not originally planned.[7]

If the exploration of potential(s) in the first part of this book has demonstrated that the concept of potential allows us to embrace a paradigm shift that assesses the essential feature of architecture based on what this item is capable of doing rather than how it has traditionally been characterized and the embedded energy as a malleable stage of matter and space, then this exploration in terms of physical transformations only outlines a mutual set of relationships between time, space, and matter across adaptive reuse processes. Applying a phenomenological approach, this potential is mainly explored in the moment before the adaptation and at the times of (de)constructive actions, as the diagram below outlines.

Comparative tables have shown that the transformative potential as framed through the methodology assumes a value in a *comparative perspective* only. It is itself a methodological attempt to join the morphology development in terms of "deformation" and in (de)constructive actions. The transformative potential that emerged from this analysis is not a parameter, and not an index or a formula. It is an open relationship that outlines a trajectory of the evolution of form. Some of these trajectories share a common tendency, which allows to cluster them into macro types of potential related to adaptive reuse projects.

It is a matter of fact that the relationship between existing and new within the transformation process includes *deconstructive* processes as well. Each arrow represents a deformation level in terms of layer, which includes "unfinished" buildings with an incomplete set of layers.

However, attempting a definition of transformative potentials in terms of "attitudes" that some transformations have underlined, the findings allow us to delineate macro types of transformative potential.

The book proposes four kinds of transformative potentials as the interplay between these three elements: decay, actions, and energy flow: 1) *palliative* potential; 2) *integrative* potential; 3) *additive* potential; and 4) *highly additive* potential.

Proposed clusters bring together the variations in terms of "relative completeness" expressed by "layers as found," the impact of the design actions, both constructive and deconstructive, and the variation of embodied energy weighted on the retroactive embodied energy, as representative of the materials' flow. In other words, it is a first attempt to define a pattern between

Embodied energy related to GSA

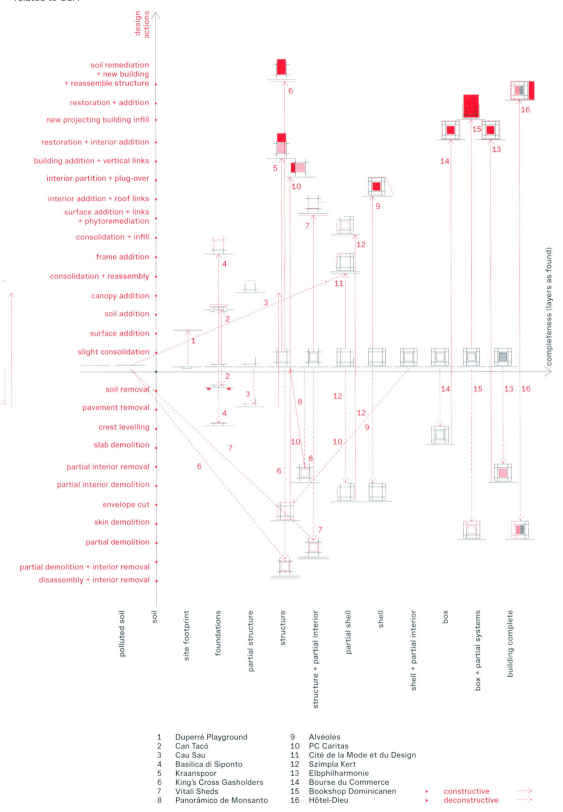

1	Duperré Playground	9	Alvéoles
2	Can Tacó	10	PC Caritas
3	Cau Sau	11	Cité de la Mode et du Design
4	Basilica di Siponto	12	Szimpla Kert
5	Kraanspoor	13	Elbphilharmonie
6	King's Cross Gasholders	14	Bourse du Commerce
7	Vitali Sheds	15	Bookshop Dominicanen
8	Panorâmico de Monsanto	16	Hôtel-Dieu

• constructive
• deconstructive

Conclusions

existing building completeness expressed in shearing layers, the intervention ordered in terms of impact on the existing building's form, and the relative variation of embodied energy between existing and adapted.

In particular, the research found that a *palliative* transformative potential is realized by means of minimal (de)constructive actions, with a low impact at the level of material variation and added embedded energy ■. [1, 7, 8, 12]

On the contrary, the *integrative transformative potential*, in terms of materials, where the transformation tends to the addition of matter, does not imply the completeness of the building in terms of shearing layers ■. [2, 3, 4]

The two *additive potentials* are characterized by their overall impact in terms of both energy flow and (de)constructional actions. Specifically, the additive potential is characterized by a marked need to undertake de(constructive) actions in the face of relative initial completeness and a weighted impact of low embodied energy ■. [5, 6, 9, 11]

The *highly additive transformative* potential intervenes on full completeness of the original artifact, and the weighted change in added materials over existing ones is large ■. [13, 15, 11, 14, 16]

These groups represent a transition from linear to non-linear causation not only by considering the capacity to impact but by including another capacity to be affected,[8] bringing together existing completeness, (de)constructive actions, and embodied energy impact in a comparative perspective. Completeness is expressed in terms of shearing layers, design interventions in terms of weighted actions and space setting, and energy impacts in terms of weighted embodied energy impact between old and new.

These transformative potentials are equally worth considering according to their strengths and weaknesses. The "palliative potential" requires minimal (de)constructive actions and embedded energy starting from uncompleted buildings in terms of layers. This potential is not actualized through the completeness of the existing; on the contrary, it delineates morphologies that are open to hosting a wide range of further design actions. Similarly, in terms of open-end transformations that happen in the cases of the "integrative potential," minimal actions involving building fragments are integrated through the high use of weighted energy. In other words, these transformations have a relatively high energy embedded in added materials and the design of a novel morphology from scarce remains through a minimal layer addition. On the other hand, the additive potential is distinguished by a strong engagement in de(constructive) actions despite relative initial completeness and a low influence of weighted embodied energy. Then, the highly additive potential is characterized by the entire completeness of the original building and a significant increase of added elements over existing ones, both in terms of layers and embodied energy.

These types of transformative potentials would require to be explored further, especially in terms of the relationship with the existing and adapted morphology, and always intended as complementary to others potentials.

Clusters of transformative potential

Palliative
Integrative

1 Duperré Playground

2 Can Tacó

7 Panorâmico de Monsanto

3 Can Sau

8 Vitali Sheds

4 Basilica di Siponto

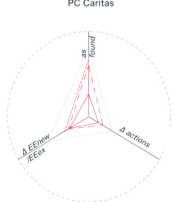

12 PC Caritas

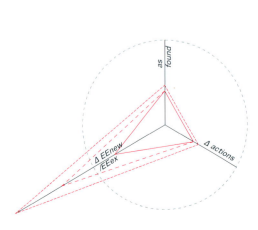

Conclusions

170

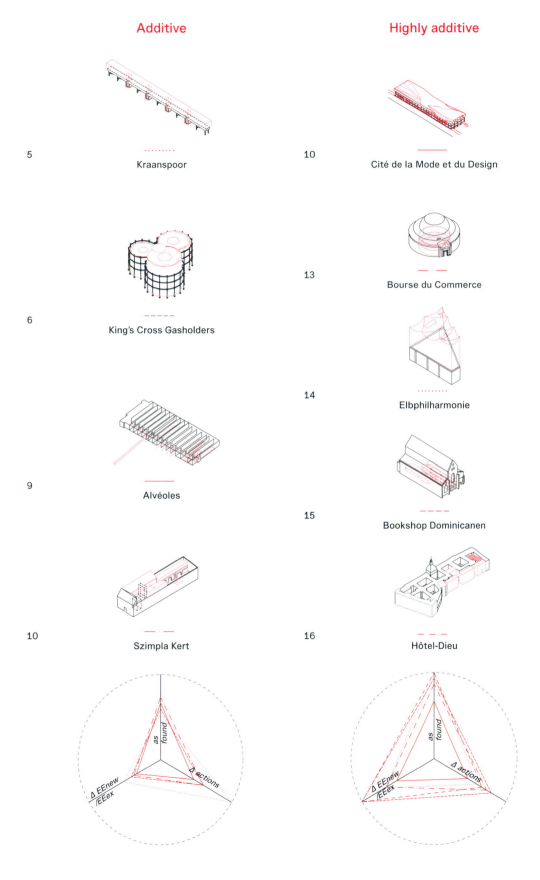

Toward sustainable forms of transformations

Final remarks and recommendations

Toward sustainable transformations of form? Some adaptive interventions are more sustainable than others, assuming that the concept of potential is, by definition, linked to a future prefiguration. The transformative potential aims to outline the adaptation trajectories of building forms. However, such a potential must consider the importance of these trajectories in terms of sustainability.[9] If sustainability is presented as "a standard against which existing institutions are to be judged and as an objective toward which society should move,"[10] some transformations are more beneficial than others.

Specifically, a form could be sustainable if it "does not diminish the opportunities of future persons to enjoy it."[11] In this context, it might be interpreted that the development of a building's form is sustainable if it embraces more possibilities than it was found with and allows for modifications in the future. Moreover, a sustainable transformation of the building's form conserves most of the resources in situ and reduces the relative amount of new resources (embodied energy flow related to materials).

However, some invasive actions are required to remediate compromised situations that may endanger future users, such as the remediation of soil pollution. Therefore, it is not solely about the number of materials employed or the action carried out but also about the type of material itself and how these actions concur with the transformation.

Sustainability might also be assumed in terms of actions, overruling the previous orders of constructive and deconstructive actions on the buildings' original form.

What if instead of measuring energies, degree of modifications, and capability to adapt in general, we retrace some trajectories that show a non-linear pattern of adaptive reuse possibilities? In doing so, transformative potentials are not defined in terms of the number of indexes, but they are defined in terms of the development trajectories of forms through a set of actions that are both constructive and deconstructive and are roughly clustered in four families (palliative, integrative, additive, highly additive).

We should outline some additional findings that emerged from this exploration. First, buildings' changes are not just realized through constructive processes, because they usually require deconstructive phases, and stages of relative completeness are equally relevant in the adaptation of buildings. Most cases have shown deconstructive phases. However, it is a fact that with fragments of existing buildings, any adaptive project has applied highly deconstructive approaches, both in terms of layers and materials. Starting from fragments, these projects always tend to conserve what is presented.

Second, decay stages in terms of layer (in)completeness have shown a strong correlation to design actions only if such actions are considered to be related to a specific morphology. In the sample analyzed, the morphologies are too heterogeneous to delineate general assumptions in terms of transformative potential. The attempt to define the cross-relationship between old and new so as to be generalizable would require a larger sample.

In fact, the additional "examples" and "unexpected" cases prefigurate a further in-depth analysis.

However, a series of existing/transformed morphologies has emerged in each case: 1) urban enclosure/open urban box; 2) isolated track/platform circuit; 3) spine walls/urban nook; 4) foundation/ideal frame; 5) platform/elevated box; 6) container frame/caged cylinder; 7) shed frame/open canopy; 8) round plates/panoramic exoskeleton; 9) clustered slab/incremental stripe hub; 10) grid block/infilled modular box; 11) ruin shell/active courtyard ruin; 12) pavilion under demolition/multilayer square; 13) rotunda/multilevel ring; 14) tripartite shed/interior panoramic shelf; 15) polygonal box/overflowing building; 16) polymorph courtyard block/permeable courtyard block. These morphologies might be explored in-depth, applying a methodological approach similar to this work but focusing on analogous existing morphologies, to highlight a more accurate pattern in deformations.

Third, embodied energy and construction material flows play a crucial role in defining the potential for transformation in light of the sustainable use of resources. In fact, we can say that some transformations are more sustainable than others. Assuming that the concept of potential is by definition linked to a future prefiguration, this potential might take trajectories more sustainable than others. This sustainable use of resources refers not only to additions and demolitions required to adapt a building but also to assessing a hierarchy of conservation of existing buildings. Some buildings, even if they have lost their functional purpose, might be worth being conserved in terms of energy embedded in their original materials still in place. The retroactive embodied energy and its impact in the field of building adaptation should gain much more attention and study. I hope this work can help in that matter.

Fourth, the methodological approach of this research is ready to be applied to further comparative analysis between a more homogeneous sample. Assuming that the completeness of layers is not always to be achieved through adaptive reuse projects, the integrated methodology proposed here aims to be functional by being aligned and specified in adaptive reuse theory, and finally to have an impact on the evaluation of existing buildings to foster the acceptance of a broader range of design solutions.

The transformative potential as framed in this research would be quantifiable in comparative terms only, by being tested on a large and morphologically homogeneous sample and establishing a scope of this potential. Further research to expand the depth of this topic is therefore suggested, following three complementary directions: 1) enlarging the sample of projects for comparative consideration; 2) analyzing similar morpho-structural types, or in other words, buildings that share similar structural rhythms and dimensions; 3) assuming a goal-oriented approach, for instance, to boost transformative potential(s) in terms of environmental sustainability.

To conclude, this journey to explore the potential(s) of form is just a first step toward an integrated approach that aims to evaluate the existing building stock transformed in terms of form to highlight best practices according to decay levels assumed as unavoidable in the existing building fabric. In doing so, a shift is made from a typology framework to a morphology framework as it is able to foster a sustainable approach to building adaptations by working on transformative patterns rather than the dichotomy between old and new.

GLOSSARY RELATING TO POTENTIAL

This concise glossary represents a vocabulary of the transformative potential as a concept of adaptive reuse.

Adaptive reuse:
any process of reusing an obsolete and derelict building by changing its function to maximize the reuse and preservation of existing materials and structures according to the design intervention to meet changing users' needs.

Building:
the result of assembling materials into a structure. (Whitney and Benjamin 1901) All structures are potential buildings. Specifically, buildings might be seen as assemblages of materials that give shelter to human life, enabling it to fulfil a functional purpose.

Concept:
a precursor to constructs in making sense of organizational worlds where researchers investigate them or theorists work on modeling them. (Gioia et al. 2012, 16)

Conservation:
assuming a goal-oriented definition, it is the actions on existing objects that aim to adapt and reuse them. (Ashworth 2011, 13)

Decay:
the evolution of a designed object from its initial "completeness" to a stage where either time, nature, non-architects, or non-human beings have affected the initial completeness and added other occasional layers. (Desilvey 2017) Specifically, "decay" is here considered a "physical decay," "deterioration," or "absolute obsolescence." (Abramson 2016; Buitelaar et al. 2021)

Form:
a twofold structuring of matter and space, or what architects refer to as the full and the empty. (Borie et al. 1978) In other words, it is the point of contact between mass and space. (Bacon 1967, 16)

Function:
uses and activities that a building is meant to host. It relies on the Vitruvian concept of *utilitas*. (Pollio and Gwilt 1874)

Inductive approach:
reasoning that starts with observations and moves toward more abstract generalizations and ideas. The inductive approach might start from intuition but not from a fixed hypothesis. (Gioia et al. 2012, 16)

Intervention:
the act of interfering with the outcome or course, especially of a condition or process. In other words, "the action of becoming intentionally

involved in a difficult situation, to improve it or prevent it from getting worse."[12] In the adaptation of buildings, an intervention is the design act that modifies the original form to allow an existing building to host a new use. (Douglas 2006)

Massing:
a unified composition of three-dimensional volumes that gives the impression of weight, density, and bulk; (Ching 1979, 430) in other words, "the perceptually dominant three-dimensional configuration of a building." (Clark and Pause 1985, 4)

Morphology:
the study of form, or the history of variation in form. (Goethe et al. 1863) In urban design, the term is principally used for "… a method of analysis which is basic to find[ing] out principles or rules of urban design." (Gebauer and Samue 1981) Here, the term means the study of the physical and spatial characteristics of a building.

Phenomenological approach:
an approach that explores a phenomenon at the time it occurs, evaluating it ex-post. (Moran 2000) Here, buildings are not inscribed in the process that has shaped them into a historical framework; on the contrary, they are perceived through their physical features as experienced when transformed.

Post-functional:
1) not being included in the function-driven paradigm on purpose—i.e., mixed-used, temporary use—or chance—i.e., buildings with any current use; 2) sites and buildings used differently than originally planned; 3) residual traces of existing sites and buildings not being used for any specific functional purpose. Such a situation is undeniable for dismissed buildings. Post-functional is the contemporary condition of the European building stock.

Preservation:
assuming a goal-oriented definition, it is the action on existing objects that aims to retain as much as possible. (Ashworth 2011, 13) In contemporary architecture debate, it might mean the saving retreat of architecture, the formless substitution that creates relevance without new form. (Koolhaas et al. 2014)

Structure:
the arrangement of parts in relation to each other and to the whole. (Eco 1980) The structure is generally associated with configuration or constitution. (Marshall 2005, 293) In architecture, it relates to the structural system only. It is "synonymous with support. […] it can be used to define the space of architecture." (Clark and Pause 1985, 3)

Sustainability:
the ability to produce balanced changes in the exploitation of primary resources, in the economic models, in the direction of technological development and institutional development, and at the same time ensure the satisfaction of current and future human needs and aspirations. (World Commission on Environment and Development 1987) Here, it refers to primary resources in terms of construction materials and to the degree of change that

the building can accomplish in terms of form.

Tendency:
the space of possibility. (DeLanda 2002) Here, it means the evolution of an object through a specific degree of freedom toward a stable, temporary stage.

Transformwative:
an adjective that means "causing a major change to something or someone, especially in a way that makes it or them better."[13] Transformative might be perceived as a degree of change in a structure. (Chomsky 1965) In architecture, it refers to conservation, adaptation, and renovation in existing buildings.[14]

Type:
in Weberian terms, it is the correlation of traits and elements of the provided phenomenon, but it is not intended to conform to all of the qualities of any specific example. It is used in the meaning of "ideal type" that "is formed by the one-sided accentuation of one or more points of view and by the synthesis of a great many diffuse, discrete, more or less present and occasionally absent concrete individual phenomena, which are arranged according to those one-sidedly emphasized viewpoints into a unified analytical construct." (Weber et al. 1949, 90)

Urban legacy:
built environment inherited from the past, including various forms of remnants, traces, materials, residual spaces, and potentially encompassing positive and negative values. It may rely on the concept of patrimonial belonging. (Lowenthal 2014) Here, the term is applied to the physical remains within the city in the form of buildings and urban sites.

Endnotes

1. Urs Fischer also presented this 1:1 scale replica of Giambologna's statue at the 54th Venice Biennale in 2011. The ephemeral representation of a human body is presented in Cristina Baldacci, Bodies of Stone in the Media, Visual Culture and the Arts, edited by A. Violi, B. Grespi, A. Pinotti, and P. Conte, 179–88 (Amsterdam University Press, 2020), https://doi.org/10.1515/9789048527069-012.
2. See the website www.atlasofpotential.com and the interactive map embedded.
3. The tables of the full process of calculating embodied energy are available online at: to be decided. It is important to mention that the values previously published by the author in her PhD thesis (Guidetti, 2022) have been revised and corrected.
4. In (DeLanda 2002), it is the potential that universal singularities are supposed to explain. Roughly, this concept is applied here to the dynamics of materials in adaptive reuse processes, even if it represents an extreme simplification within the broad concept of the virtual as the stage where infinite options coexist that might produce an actualization through a self-organizing capacity.
5. According to DeLanda, Deleuze substituted dynamic processes for entity essences, some of which are material and energetic but all of which remain immanent to the world of matter and energy. (DeLanda 2002)
6. Assuming 9,814 GWh per year, according to the official website of the Municipality of Rome, data based on 2019.
7. (Gould and Vrba 1982, 6)
8. For instance, shifting the focus from the load's ability to push to a specific material's tendency to be pushed. (DeLanda 2002)
9. Sustainability means 1) the quality of being able to continue over a period of time; 2) the quality of causing little or no damage to the environment and therefore be able to continue for a long time. Definition of sustainability from the Cambridge Advanced Learner's Dictionary & Thesaurus, Cambridge University Press. Available at https://dictionary.cambridge.org/dictionary/english/sustainability. Accessed in January 2022.
10. Meadowcroft, J., "sustainability." Encyclopaedia Britannica, January 27, 2022. https://www.britannica.com/science/sustainability.
11. Ibid.
12. "Intervention" in Cambridge dictionary, online version. Available at https://dictionary.cambridge.org/dictionary/english/intervention. Accessed in January 2022.
13. Cambridge Dictionary [Internet]. 2021. Analogy; [cited November 8, 2021]. Available at https://dictionary.cambridge.org/dictionary/english/transformative.
14. A short description of this exhibition is published [online] at https://www.pavillon-arsenal.com/en/expositions/9610-transformative-architecture.html.

REFERENCES

AAA Potential(s): Ancestry, Architecture, and Adaptations

Abenia, Tiphaine. 2017. "Dispositif de Catégorisation Des Grandes Structures En Suspens." In *Du Potentiel Des Grandes Structures Urbaines Abandonnées / On the Potential of Abandoned Large Urban Structures*, Potential Architecture Books. Vol. 01. Research Notebooks.

Abramson, Daniel M. 2016. *Obsolescence: An Architectural History*. University of Chicago Press.

Advisory Council on Historical Preservation (ACHP). 1979. *Assessing the Energy Conservation Benefits of Historic Preservation: Method and Examples*.

Agamben, Giorgio. 2013. *Opus Dei: An Archaeology of Duty*. Stanford University Press.

Alberti, L.B., G. Orlandi, and P. Portoghesi. 1966. *L'Architettura (De Re Aedificatoria) Testo Latino e Traduzione a Cura Di Giovanni Orlandi*.

Alterazioni Video and Fosbury Architecture. 2018. *Incompiuto: La Nascita Di Uno Stile*. Humboldt Books.

Amiri, Elina. 2019. "Methods to Read Adaptive Reuse Strategies and Capacities in Industrial Buildings." Master thesis, Corso di laurea magistrale in Architettura Per Il Progetto Sostenibile. Supervisors: Matteo Robiglio, Elena Guidetti, Politecnico di Torino.

Arge, Kirsten. 2005. "Adaptable Office Buildings: Theory and Practice." *Facilities* 23 (3/4): 119–127. https://doi.org/10.1108/02632770510578494/full/html.

Askar, Rand, Luís Bragança, and Helena Gervásio. 2021. "Adaptability of Buildings: A Critical Review on the Concept Evolution." *Applied Sciences* 11 (10). https://doi.org/10.3390/app11104483.

Augé, Marc, and A. Serafini. 2003. *Le Temps En Ruines*. Lignes Fictives. Galilée.

Bacon, Edmund N. 1967. *Design of Cities*. Viking Press.

Barthes, Roland. 2002. *Le neutre : notes de cours au Collège de France, 1977–1978*. Institut Mémoires de l'édition Contemporaine, Collège de France. Seuil IMEC.

———. 2019. "Kairòs." In *Kronos e Kairos*, 37–44. Electa.

Benjamin, D.N. 2017. *Embodied Energy and Design: Making Architecture Between Metrics and Narratives*. Columbia University GSAPP.

Bergevoet, T., and M. van Tuijl. 2016. *The Flexible City: Sustainable Solutions for a Europe in Transition*. nai010 publishers.

Bergson, Henri, and A. Mitchell. 1911. *Creative Evolution*. H. Holt.

Besancon, R. M. 1974. *The Encyclopedia of Physics*. Van Nostrand Reinhold. J.

Betsky, A., and E. Adigard. 2000. *Architecture Must Burn*. Gingko.

Bille, M., and T.F. Sorensen. 2016. *Elements of Architecture: Assembling Archaeology, Atmosphere and the Performance of Building Spaces*. Archaeological Orientations. Taylor & Francis.

Birgisdottir, H., A. Moncaster, A. Houlihan Wiberg, C. Chae, K. Yokoyama, M. Balouktsi, S. Seo, T. Oka, T. Lützkendorf, and T. Malmqvist. 2017. "IEA EBC Annex 57 'Evaluation of Embodied Energy and CO2eq for Building Construction.'" *Energy and Buildings* 154: 72–80. https://doi.org/10.1016/j.enbuild.2017.08.030.

Bloch, Oscar. 1975. *Dictionnaire étimologique de la langue française / Oscar Bloch, Walther von Wartburg*. 6. ed. PUF.

Bogoliubov, N.N., and D.V. Shirkov. 1959. *Introduction to the Theory of Quantized Fields*. John Wiley & Sons.

Bollack, Françoise A. 2013. *Old Buildings, New Forms: New Directions in Architectural Transformations*. Monacelli.

Borie, A., Pierre Micheloni, and Pierre Pinon. 1978. *Forme et Déformation Des Objets Architecturaux et Urbains. Eupalinos*. Parentheses Eds.

Brand, S. 1995. *How Buildings Learn: What Happens After They're Built*. Penguin Publishing Group.

———. 2000. *The Clock of the Long Now: Time and Responsibility*. "A" Phoenix Paperback.

Brooker, G. 2021. *50|50 Words for Reuse*. Canadian Press.

Brooker, G, and S. Stone. 2004. *Rereadings: Interior Architecture and the Design Principles of Remodelling Existing Buildings*. RIBA Enterprises.

———. 2019. *Re-Readings: 2: Interior Architecture and the Principles of Remodelling Existing Buildings*. RIBA Publishing.

Buitelaar, Edwin, Stefano Moroni, and Anita De Franco. 2021. "Building Obsolescence in the Evolving City. Reframing Property Vacancy and Abandonment in the Light of Urban Dynamics and Complexity." *Cities* 108 (January): 102964. https://doi.org/10.1016/j.cities.2020.102964.

Bunge, E., and M. Hoang. 2019. *Buildings and Almost Buildings: NARCHITECTS*. Actar.

Butt, Talib E., M. Camilleri, P. Paul, and K. Jones. 2015. "Obsolescence Types and the Built Environment - Definitions and Implications." *International Journal of Environment and Sustainable Development*, 14(1): 20. https://doi.org/10.1504/IJESD.2015.066896.

Byard, P.S. 2005. *The Architecture of Additions: Design and Regulation*. Norton.

Caballero Lobera, A. 2017. "Durand, Guadet and Wagner. The Evolution of the Compositive Method between 19th and 20th Century." *FAmagazine* 39 (March). https://doi.org/10.12838/issn.20390491/n39.2017/3.

Cairns, S., and J.M. Jacobs. 2014. *Buildings Must Die: A Perverse View of Architecture*. MIT Press.

Cambridge University. 2024a. "Meaning of 'Chance' in English." In *Cambridge English Dictionary*. Online: Cambridge University Press & Assessment.

———. 2024b. "Meaning of 'Deformation' in English." In *Cambridge English Dictionary*. Online: Cambridge University Press & Assessment.

———. 2024c. "Meaning of 'Latency' in English." In *Cambridge English Dictionary*. Online: Cambridge University Press & Assessment.

———. 2024d. "Meaning of 'Transformative' in English." In *Cambridge English Dictionary*. Online: Cambridge University Press & Assessment.

Carnicero, I., and C. Quintáns. 2018. *Unfinished: Ideas, Images, and Projects from the Spanish Pavilion at the 15th Venice Architecture Biennale*. Actar.

Ching, F.D.K. 1979. *Architecture: Form, Space, and Order*. 1st ed. Van Nostrand Reinhold.

Chomsky, N. 1965. *Aspects of the Theory of Syntax*. Cambridge: MIT Press.

Christ, C. F. 1968. "Input-Output Economics. Wassily Leontief." *The Journal of Political Economy* 76 (6): 1247–49. https://doi.org/10.1086/259488.

Christopher, Matthew. 2016. *Abandoned America: Dismantling the Dream*. Carpet Bombing Culture.

Chupin, J., and T. Abenia. 2017. *Du Potential Des Grandes Structures Urbaine Abandonnes / On the Potential of Abandoned Large Urban Structures*. Potential Architecture Books.

Clark, Roger. H., and M. Pause. 1985. *Precedents in Architecture: Analytic Diagrams, Formative Ideas, and Partis*. Wiley.

Corbellini, G. 2016. *Exlibris. 16 Parole Chiave Dell'architettura Contemporanea*. LetteraVentidue.

Cormen, Thomas H., Charles E. Leiserson, Ronald L. Rivest, and Clifford Stein. 2001. *The Potential Method. Introduction to Algorithms (2nd Ed.)*. MIT Press and McGraw-Hill.

Corner, J. 2002. "The Agency of Mapping: Speculation, Critique and Invention." In *Mappings*. Reaktion.

Dardi, C. 1987. "Contenitori Storici: Limiti Della Flessibilità." In *Perego F. (a Cura Di) Anastilosi. L'antico, Il Restauro, La Città*. Laterza. http://ffmaam.it/pubblicazioni/anastilosi-1986.

Darwin, C., J. Murray, W. Clowes and Sons, and Bradbury & Evans. 1859. *On the Origin of Species by Means of Natural Selection, Or, The Preservation of Favoured Races in the Struggle for Life*. The World's Classics. J. Murray.

De Paris, S., and C. Nuno Lopes. 2018. "Housing Flexibility Problem: Review of Recent Limitations and Solutions." *Frontiers of Architectural Research* 7 (March). https://doi.org/10.1016/j.foar.2017.11.004.

DeLanda, M. 2002. *Intensive Science and Virtual Philosophy*. Series Editor. Bloomsbury Academic.

DeLanda, M., J. Protevi, and T. Thanem. 2005. "Deleuzian Interrogations: A Conversation with Manuel DeLanda, John Protevi and Torkild Thanem." *Tamara: Critical Journal of Postmodern Organization Science* 3 (December): 65–88.

Deleuze, G. 1988. *Bergsonism*. Zone Books.

Deleuze, G, and F. Guattari. 1987. *A Thousand Plateaus: Capitalism and Schizophrenia*. University of Minnesota Press.

Desilvey, C. 2017. *Curated Decay: Heritage Beyond Saving*. University of Minnesota Press.

DeSilvey, C., H. Fredheim, H. Fluck, R. Hails, R. Harrison, I. Samuel, and A. Blundell. 2021. "When Loss Is More: From Managed Decline to Adaptive Release." *The Historic Environment: Policy & Practice* 12 (3–4): 418–33. https://doi.org/10.1080/17567505.2021.1957263.

DeSilvey, C., and R. Harrison. 2020. "Anticipating Loss: Rethinking Endangerment in Heritage Futures." *International Journal of Heritage Studies* 26 (1): 1–7. https://doi.org/10.1080/13527258.2019.1644530.

Dermot M. 2000. *Introduction to Phenomenology*, ch. 6. Routledge.

Douglas, J. 2006. *Building Adaptation*. Butterworth-Heinemann.

Duffy, F. 1992. *The Changing Workplace*. Phaidon Press.

Duignan, B. 2019. "Plato and Aristotle: How Do They Differ?" In *Encyclopedia Britannica*, Online.

Durand, J-N-L., and J. G. Legrand. 1801. "Recueil et parallèle des édifices de tout genre anciens et modern, remarquables par leur beauté, par leur grandeur, ou par leur singularité, et dessinés sur une même échelle." https://doi.org/10.11588/diglit.1608.

Eck, C. van. 1998. "The Structure of 'De Re Aedificatoria' Reconsidered." *Journal of the Society of Architectural Historians* 57 (3): 280–97. https://doi.org/10.2307/991347.

Eco, U. 1962. *Opera Aperta: Forma e Indeterminazione Nelle Poetiche Contemporanee*. Delfini-Cultura. Bompiani.

———. 1979. *The Role of the Reader: Explorations in the Semiotics of Texts*. Advances in Semiotics. Indiana University Press.

———. 1980. *La Struttura Assente*. Tascabili Bompiani. Bompiani.

———. 1984. *Semiotics and the Philosophy of Language*. Advances in Semiotics. Indiana University Press.

Eldredge, N., and S. Gould. 1971. "Punctuated Equilibria: An Alternative to Phyletic Gradualism." In *Models in Paleobiology*, 82: 82–115.

Ellen, L.A. van, B.N. Bridgens, N. Burford, and O. Heidrich. 2021. "Rhythmic Buildings – a Framework for Sustainable Adaptable Architecture." *Building and Environment* 203 (October): 108068. https://doi.org/10.1016/j.buildenv.2021.108068.

Engel, H. 1981. *Tragsysteme: Structure Systems*. [S.l.]: [s.n.].

Etymonline. 2024. "Potential." In *Online Etymology Dictionary*. Etymonline Repository.

Fabian, L., E. Giannotti, and P. Viganò. 2012. *Recycling City. Lifecycles, Embodied Energy, Inclusion*. Giavedoni.

Farrell, Y., and S. McNamara. 2018. *Freespace: Biennale Architettura 2018: Short Guide*. La Biennale di Venezia.

Feynman, R.P., R. B. Leighton, and M. L. Sands. 1963. *The Feynman Lectures on Physics*. Addison-Wesley Pub. Co.

Fisher-Gewirtzman, D. 2016. "Adaptive Reuse Architecture Documentation and Analysis." *Journal of Architectural Engineering Technology* 5 (January). https://doi.org/10.4172/2168-9717.1000172.

Fluck, H., and Meredith W. 2017. "Climate Change, Heritage Policy and Practice in England: Risks and Opportunities." https://doi.org/10.17863/CAM.23646.

Frampton, K., J. Cava, Graham Foundation for Advanced Studies in the Fine Arts. 1995. *Studies in Tectonic Culture : The Poetics of Construction in Nineteenth and Twentieth Century Architecture*. MIT Press.

Françoise, J.P., G.L. Naber, and S.T. Tsou. 2006. *Encyclopedia of Mathematical Physics*. V. 3. Elsevier.

Friedman, Y. 2000. "Function Follows Form." In *Non-Plan*, 104–13. Routledge.

Fujimoto, S. 2008. *Primitive Future*. Inax Pub.

Galilei, G. 1638. *Discorsi e Dimostrazioni Matematiche Intorno a Due Nuove Scienze*. Ludovico Elzeviro.

Gann, D. M., and James Barlow. 1996. "Flexibility in Building Use: The Technical Feasibility of Converting Redundant Offices into Flats." *Construction Management and Economics* 14 (1): 55–66.

Gaspar, P. Lima, and A. Lobato Santos. 2015. "Embodied Energy on Refurbishment vs. Demolition: A Southern Europe Case Study." *Energy and Buildings* 87 (January): 386–94. https://doi.org/10.1016/j.enbuild.2014.11.040.

Gausa, M., and Instituto Metápolis de Arquitectura Avanzada. 2003. *The Metapolis Dictionary of Advanced Architecture: City, Technology and Society in the Information Age*. Actar.

Gauss, C.F. 2009. *General Investigations of Curved Surfaces of 1827 and 1825*. Fite Press.

Geraedts, R. 2016. "FLEX 4.0, A Practical Instrument to Assess the Adaptive Capacity of Buildings." *Sustainable Built Environment Tallinn and Helsinki Conference SBE16*. Vol. 96 (September): 568–79. https://doi.org/10.1016/j.egypro.2016.09.102.

Geraedts, R., M. Hermans, H. Remøy, and E. Rijn. 2014. *Adaptive Capacity Of Buildings – A Determination Method to Promote Flexible and Sustainable Construction*. https://doi.org/10.13140/2.1.4568.8961.

Geraedts, R., and M. Prins. 2015. *The CE Meter; An Instrument to Assess the Circular Economy Capacity of Buildings*.

Gebauer, M. and I. Samuels. 1981. *Urban Morphology: An Introduction*, Joint Centre for Urban Design, Research Note 8. Oxford Polytechnic.

Giedion, S. 1954. *Space, Time, and Architecture: The Growth of a New Tradition*. Harvard University Press.

———. 1982. "The Evolution of New Potentialities." In *Space, Time and Architecture*, 163–290. The Growth of a New Tradition, Fifth revised and enlarged Edition. Harvard University Press. https://doi.org/10.2307/j.ctv1bzfnzf.10.

Goethe J.W. von, B., Mueller, C.J., Engard. 1952. *Goethe's Botanical Writings*. University of Hawai'i Press.

Goethe, J.W. von. 1790. *Versuch Die Metamorphose Der Pflanzen Zu Erklären*. Ettinger.

Goethe, R., E.M. Cox, and M.T. Masters. 1863. *Goethe's Essay on the Metamorphosis of Plants*. J.E. Taylor.

Gosling, J., P. Sassi, M. Naim, and R. Lark. 2013. "Adaptable Buildings: A Systems Approach." *Sustainable Cities and Society* 7 (July): 44–51. https://doi.org/10.1016/j.scs.2012.11.002.

Gould, S. J., and Elisabeth S. Vrba. 1982. "Exaptation-A Missing Term in the Science of Form." *Paleobiology* 8 (1): 4–15.

Grammenos, F., and P. Russell. 1997. "Building Adaptability : A View from the Future."

Green, G. 1828. *An Essay on the Application of Mathematical Analysis to the Theories of Electricity and Magnetism*. Wezäta-Melins 1958.

Groak, S. 2002. *The Idea of Building: Thought and Action in the Design and Production of Buildings*. Taylor & Francis.

Guidetti, E., and M. Ferrara. 2023. "Embodied Energy in Existing Buildings as a Tool for Sustainable Intervention on Urban Heritage." *Sustainable Cities and Society* 88 (January): 104284. https://doi.org/10.1016/j.scs.2022.104284.

Gurisatti, G. 2019. "Pensare le costellazioni. Critica della storia storia critica di Nietzsche e Benjamin." In *Kronos e Kairos*, 57–73. Electa.

Habraken, N. J. 2000. *The Structure of the Ordinary: Form and Control in the Built Environment*. MIT Press.

Habraken, N. J. 1991. *Supports: An Alternative to Mass Housing*. 2nd edition, reprint of the 1972 English edition. Urban International Press.

Hacking, I. 1990. *The Taming of Chance*. Ideas in Context. Cambridge University Press. https://books.google.it/books?id=KffZAQAAQBAJ.

Hammond, C.P., and C.I. Jones. 2011. *Inventory of Carbon and Energy (ICE), Beta Version V2.0*. Department of Engineering, University of Bath.

Heath, T. 1989. "Lessons from Vitruvius." *Design Studies* 10 (4): 246–53. https://doi.org/10.1016/0142-694X(89)90008-2.

Hertzberger, H., L. Ghaït, and I. Rike. 2005. *Lessons for Students in Architecture*. 010 Publishers. https://books.google.it/books?id=l7KxKAAHW2sC.

Hill, J. 2019. *The Architecture of Ruins: Designs on the Past, Present and Future*. Taylor & Francis. https://books.google.it/books?id=tvWODwAAQBAJ.

Hirsch H.G. 1997. "Webers Idealtypus Als Methode Zur Bestimmung Des Begriffsinhaltes Theoretischer Begriffe in Den Kulturwissenschaften." *Journal for General Philosophy of Science* 28 (2): 275–96. https://doi.org/10.1023/A:1008207612359.

Holtorf, C. 2015. "Averting Loss Aversion in Cultural Heritage." *International Journal of Heritage Studies* 21 (4): 405–21. https://doi.org/10.1080/13527258.2014.938766.

Huges, J. 2000. "The Indeterminate Building." In *NON-PLAN. Essays on Freedom Participation and Change in Modern Architecture and Urbanism*, Architectural Press, 90–103. Routledge.

Hughes, J., and S. Sadler. 2000. *Non-Plan: Essays on Freedom Participation and Change in Modern Architecture and Urbanism*. Architectural Press.

Hurol, Y. 2015. *The Tectonics of Structural Systems: An Architectural Approach*. Taylor & Francis.

Jackson, M. 2005. "Embodied Energy and Historic Preservation: A Needed Reassessment." *APT Bulletin: The Journal of Preservation Technology* 36 (4): 47–52.

Jullien, F., and J. Lloyd. 2004. *A Treatise on Efficacy*. English edition. University of Hawai'i Press.

Jullien, F. 1992. *La Propension Des Choses. Pour Une Histoire de l'efficacité En Chine*. Seuil.

———. 2002. *Traité de l'efficacité*. Biblios Essais. Grasset.

———. 2005. *Conférénce Sur l'efficacité*. Presses universitaires de France.

Kendall, S. 1999. *Open Building: An Approach to Sustainable Architecture*. Vol. 6. https://doi.org/10.1080/10630739983551.

Koolhaas, R., J. Otero-Pailos, M. Wigley, and J. Carver. 2014. *Preservation Is Overtaking Us*. GSAPP Transcripts. GSAPP Books. https://books.google.it/books?id=jVGIoAEACAAJ.

Koolhaas, R. 1995. "The Generic City." In *S, M, L, XL*, 1948–94. The Monacelli Press.

Koolhaas, R., and B. Mau. 1998. *S, M, L, XL: Office for Metropolitan Architecture*. 2nd ed. The Monacelli press.

Kuipers, M. C., and W. de Jonge. 2017. *Designing from Heritage: Strategies for Conservation and Conversion*. TU Delft – Heritage & Architecture.

Kurrent, F. 1978. *Architettura Moderna in Ambienti Storici*, Bayerische Architektenkammer. Die Neue Sammlung.

Langston, C. 2012. "Validation of the Adaptive Reuse Potential (ARP) Model Using iconCUR." *Facilities* 30 (3/4): 105–23. https://doi.org/10.1108/02632771211202824.

Langston, C., E. Hiu-Kwan Yung, and E. Hon-Wan Chan. 2013. "The Application of ARP Modelling to Adaptive Reuse Projects in Hong Kong." *Habitat International* 40 (October): 233–43. https://doi.org/10.1016/j.habitatint.2013.05.002.

Larousse. 1971. *La grande encyclopédie*. Vol. 16. Librairie Larousse.

Latour, A. 1991. "Remarks, 1965." In *Louis Kahn: Writings, Lectures, Interviews*, 197–219. Rizzoli.

Leaman, A., B. Bordass, and S. Cassels. 1998. "Flexibility and Adaptability in Buildings: The 'Killer' Variables." London: Building Use Studies.

Leupen, B. 2006. *Frame and Generic Space : A Study into the Changeable Dwelling, Proceeding from the Permanent*. 010 Publishers.

Lin, T-Y., and S.D. Stotesbury. 1988. *Structural Concepts and Systems for Architects and Engineers*. Van Nostrand Reinhold Co.

Lucas, G., 2012. *Understanding the Archaeological Record*. Cambridge University Press.

Luhmann, N. 1995. *Social Systems*. Timothy Lenoir and Hons Ulrich Gumbreeht. Stanford University Press.

Maddex, D., and National Trust for Historic Preservation in the United States. 1981. *New Energy from Old Buildings*. Preservation Press.

Manolopoulou, Y. 2007. "The Active Voice of Architecture: An Introduction to the Idea of Chance." *The University of Sheffield School of Architecture* field (1): 62–72.

———. 2013. *Architectures of Chance*. Design Research in Architecture. Ashgate Publishing Limited.

Mari, E. 1992. *Ecolo*. Design product for Alessi.

Martin, E. A., R. Hine, and Oxford University Press. 2008. *A Dictionary of Biology*. Oxford University Press.

Maslow, A. 1943. "A Theory of Human Motivation." *Psychological Review* 50 (4): 370–96. https://doi.org/10.1037/h0054346.

———. 2013. *Toward a Psychology of Being*. Start Publishing LLC.

Meyer, A., and S. Orlando. 1961. *Dizionario Tecnico: Italiano - Tedesco e Tedesco - Italiano: ... = Technisches Wörterbuch: ...* 2nd ed. Editore Ulrico Hoepli/Brandstetter Verlag.

Monteiro, A.C.S. 2015. "Assessing Initial Embodied Energy in Building Structures Using LCA Methodology."

Mourão, J., R. Gomes, L. Matias, and S. Niza. 2019. "Combining Embodied and Operational Energy in Buildings Refurbishment Assessment." *Energy and Buildings* 197 (August): 34–46. https://doi.org/10.1016/j.enbuild.2019.05.033.

Murray, J.A.H, H. Bradley, W.A. Craigie, and C.T. Onions. 1978. *The Oxford English Dictionary : Being a Corrected Reissue with an Introduction, Supplement, and Bibliography of A New English Dictionary on Historical Principles*. Vol. 12. Oxford University Press.

Muscato, C. 2005. "Dunamis, Arche, Kratos. Il Problema Del Potere in Platone." *Itinerari* (1).

Nencioni, G. 1987. *Vocabolario degli Accademici della Crusca*. Firenze: Le Lettere.

Newton, I. 1686. *Philosophiæ naturalis principia mathematica*. Cambridge Digital Library. *Annals of Science* 77 (3).

Norberg-Schulz, C. 1980. *Genius Loci: Towards a Phenomenology of Architecture*. Rizzoli.

OMA and R. Koolhaas. 2011. "Extreme Demolition and Extreme Preservation." *MONU* 14 (Editing Urbanism): 17–32.

O'Neill, R.V., D.L. Deangelis, J.B. Waide, and T.F.H. Allen. 2021. *A Hierarchical Concept of Ecosystems. (MPB-23)*, Volume 23. Monographs in Population Biology. Princeton University Press. https://press.princeton.edu/books/paperback/9780691084374/a-hierarchical-concept-of-ecosystems-mpb-23-volume-23.

Onions, C.T. (ed.). 1966. *The Oxford Dictionary of English Etymology*. Clarendon Press.

Picon, A. 2000. "Anxious Landscapes: From the Ruin to Rust." *Grey Room*, 64–83.

Place, J.W. 2007. "Architectural Structures." John Wiley & Sons.

Plevoets, B., and K. Van Cleempoel. 2019. *Adaptive Reuse of the Built Heritage: Concepts and Cases of an Emerging Discipline*. Routledge. https://doi.org/10.4324/9781315161440.

Poerschke, U. 2016. *Architectural Theory of Modernism: Relating Functions and Forms*. Routledge.

Pollio, M.V., and J. Gwilt. 1874. *The Architecture of Marcus Vitruvius Pollio, in Ten Books*. Weale's Scientific & Technical Series. Lockwood.

Pollio, V., M.H. Morgan, and H.L. Warren. 1914. *Vitruvius, the Ten Books on Architecture*. Harvard University Press.

Rabeneck, A., D. Sheppard. 1973. "Housing Flexibility." *Architectural Design* 43 (November): 698–732.

Rankine, W.J. 1853. *The London, Edinburgh and Dublin Philosophical Magazine and Journal of Science*. Vol. series 4: vol. 5 (January–June 1853). Taylor & Francis.

Reale, G. 2000. *Timeo. Testo Greco a Fronte*. Bompiani Testi a Fronte. Bompiani.

Reiser, J., and N. Umemoto. 2006. *Atlas of Novel Tectonics*. Princeton Architectural Press.

Ridder, H.-G. 2017. "The Theory Contribution of Case Study Research Designs." *Business Research* 10 (2): 281–305. https://doi.org/10.1007/s40685-017-0045-z.

Riegl, A. 1984. *Le culte moderne des monuments : son essence et sa geneèse*. Editions du Seuil.

Robert, P. 1989. *Reconversions, Adaptations: New Uses for Old Buildings*. Architecture Thématique. Ed. Du Moniteur.

Robiglio, M. 2017. *RE-USA, 20 American Stories of Adaptive Reuse, A Toolkit for Post-Industrial Cities*. jovis.

Rocci, L., and G. Argan. 2011. *Vocabolario greco-italiano*. Società editrice Dante Alighieri.

Rossi, A. 1981. *A Scientific Autobiography*. Oppositions Books/MIT Press.

———. 1966. "La Teoria Della Permanenza e i Monumenti." In *L' Architettura Della Città / Aldo Rossi*. Marsilio.

———. 1972. "Alternative per Un Concetto Di Monumentalità." *Casabella*, December 1972.

Rudofsky, B., and Museum of Modern Art, New York. 1987. *Architecture Without Architects: A Short Introduction to Non-Pedigreed Architecture*. University of New Mexico Press.

Ruskin, J. 1849. *The Seven Lamps of Architecture*. J. Wiley.

Sandler, D. 2016. *Counterpreservation: Architectural Decay in Berlin since 1989*. Series edited by Peter Uwe Hohendahl. 1st ed. Cornell University Press.

Scheffler, I. 1985. *Of Human Potential (Routledge Revivals): An Essay in the Philosophy of Education*. Vol. 25. Routledge & Kegan Paul.

Schmidt, R., S. Austin, and D. Brown. 2009. "Designing Adaptable Buildings."

Schneider, T., and J. Till. 2007. *Flexible Housing*. Architectural Press. https://doi.org/10.4324/9781315393582.

Semper, G. 1851. *The four elements of architecture and other writings*. Cambridge University Press.

Simmel, G. 1919. "Die Ruin." In *Philosophische Kultur. Gesammelte Essays*, [1911] 2nd, 125–33. Alfred Kröner Verlag.

Sinclair, J. 2010a. "Indeterminate." In *Collins English Dictionary*. Online: HarperCollins.

———. 2010b. "Potential." In *Collins English Dictionary*. Online: HarperCollins.

Sky, A., and M. Stone. 1983. *Unbuilt America: Forgotten Architecture in the United States from Thomas Jefferson to the Space Age : A Site Book*. A SITE Book. Abbeville Press.

Slaughter, E.S. 2001. "Design Strategies to Increase Building Flexibility." *Building Research & Information* 29 (3): 208–17.

Smith, J.E. 1969. "TIME, TIMES, AND THE 'RIGHT TIME'; 'CHRONOS' AND 'KAIROS.'" *The Monist* 53 (1): 1–13.

Stahel, W.R., and G. Reday-Mulvey. 1981. *Jobs for Tomorrow: The Potential for Substituting Manpower for Energy*. Vantage Press.

Stanley, M. 2006. "The Fun Palace as Virtual Architecture. Cedric Price and the Practices of Indeterminacy." *Journal of Architectural Education*, Hobart and William Smith Colleges: 39–48.

Sullivan, L.H. 1896. "The Tall Office Building Artistically Considered." *Lippincott's Magazine* 57, J.B. Lippincott Co: 403–09.

Sun-Tzu, and L. Giles. 1910. *The Art of the War*. Clarendon Press.

Tafuri, M. 1980. *Theories and History of Architecture*. Icon Editions. Harper & Row.

Villari, S. 1990. *J.N.L. Durand (1760-1834): Art and Science of Architecture*. Rizzoli.

Wachsmann, K. 1961. *The Turning Point of Building: Structure and Design*. Reinhold Pub. Corp.

Weber, M., E. Shils, and H.A. Finch. 1949. *The Methodology of the Social Sciences*. Free Press.

Week, J. 1966. "Indeterminate Architecture." In *The Transactions of the Bartlett Society, 1963-1964*, 2:83–106. The Bartlett School of Architecture.

White, E.T. 1999. *Path, Portal, Place. Appreciating Public Space in Urban Environments*. Architectural Media.

Wilkinson, S.J., and H. Remøy. 2011. "Sustainability and within Use Office Building Adaptations: A Comparison of Dutch and Australian Practices." Conference paper. Gold Coast: Bond University.

Wong, L. 2016. *Adaptive Reuse. Extending the Lives of Buildings*. Birkhäuser Verlag AG.

Woodward, C. 2001. *In Ruins*. Pantheon Books.

Zanatta, M. 2009. *Metafisica. Testo Greco a Fronte. Classici Greci e Latini*. Bureau Biblioteca Univ. Rizzoli.

Žižek, S. 2010. *Living in the End Times*. Verso.

AR Post-functional Forms: Adaptive Reuse Projects Through Stages of Completeness

Barasch, D. 2019. *Ruin and Redemption in Architecture*. Phaidon.

Bethenod, M., and G. Robinne. 2021. *La Bourse Du Commerce, Le Museé de La Collection Pinault à Paris – The Museum of the Pinault Collection in Paris*. éditions Dilecta.

Boie, G. 2019. "La mente sociale – The social mind." *Domus* 1036 (Tradizione istantanea-Instant heritage): 650–57.

Brunet, F. 1809. *Dimensions des fers qui doivent former la coupole de la Halle aux Grains, calculées, d'après la composition de M. Bélanger, architecte des monuments publics, par F. Brunet*. chez Firmin Didot, imprimeur-libraire, et graveur de l'imprimerie impériale.

Cambridge University. 2024a. "Meaning of 'Box' in English." In *Cambridge English Dictionary*. Online: Cambridge University Press & Assessment.

———. 2024b. "Meaning of 'Footprint' in English." In *Cambridge English Dictionary*. Online: Cambridge University Press & Assessment.

———. 2024c. "Meaning of 'Shell' in English." In *Cambridge English Dictionary*. Online: Cambridge University Press & Assessment.

———. 2024d. "Meaning of 'Structure' in English." In *Cambridge English Dictionary*. Online: Cambridge University Press & Assessment.

Cayuela, N, and Anne-Françoise Sarger. 2016. *The Grand Hôtel Dieu of Lyon*. Libel editions.

COLOCO. 2011. "Third-Landscape Gardens." 2011.

Commission de vieux Paris. 2017. "Compte-de rendu de seance." Séance plénière. Mairie de Paris.

De Vylder, J., I. Vinck, J. Taillieu, G. Boie, S. Bollaert, C. Bonte, O. Bral, et al. 2018. *Unless Ever People*. Flanders Architecture Institute.

Destombes, L. 2017. "Traductions constructives du projet d'architecture. Théoriser le détail à l'ère de la modélisation intégrative." PhD thesis. École d'architecture, Faculté de l'aménagement.

Devoldere, S., C. Grafe, J. Hill, W. Mann, L. Meganck, S. Stone, M. Van Balen, K. Van Cleempoel, and C. Voet. 2023. *As Found. Experiments in Preservation*. Edited by S. De Caigny, H. Ertas, B. Plevoets. Flanders Architecture Institute.

Figueiredo, J., and C. Martins. 2018. "O Óvni de Lisboa." *Expresso Impresa Publishing SA*.

Fitz, A., E. Krasny, and Architekturzentrum Wien. 2019. "PC Caritas, Melle, Belgium." In *Critical Care: Architecture and Urbanism for a Broken Planet*. The MIT Press. https://doi.org/10.7551/mitpress/12273.003.0033.

Gironés, T. 2021. Interview by the author with the architect in his studio in Barcelona.

Guidetti, E., and A. Massarente. 2020. "Kraanspoor: risemantizzazione di un'infrastruttura del lavoro." *BLOOM*, Opere, 30: 63–67.

———. 2021. "Configurations, Deformations, Mutations. Criteria of Morphological Analysis in Adaptive Reuse." *AGATHÓN | International Journal of Architecture, Art and Design* 9 (online). https://doi.org/10.19229/2464-9309/982021.

Hovens, F., M. Monteiro, K. Schutgens, et al. 2006. *Dominicanen Geschiedenis van Kerk En Klooster in Maastricht*. Stichting Historische Reeks Maastricht.

Kleilein, D. 2018. "Psychiatrie in Gent." *Bauwelt* 9 (September).

Kostka, G., and J. Fiedler. 2016. *Large Infrastructure Projects in Germany: Between Ambition and Realities*. Palgrave MacMillan.

Lecardane, R., and Z. Tesoriere. 2011. "Cultural Bunker: The Regeneration of Urban Military Heritage in Saint-Nazaire." *In Situ* 16. https://doi.org/10.4000/insitu.779.

LIN Architects. 2007. "Alveole 14 Saint-Nazaire, France." https://www.lin-a.com/sites/default/files/SNA-PDF_0.pdf.

Mack, G., Herzog & de Meuron. 2018. *Herzog & de Meuron Elbphilharmonie Hamburg*. Birkhäuser.

Metz, T. 2011. "Kraanspoor, Amsterdam, OTH." *Architectural Records*, BTS Restoration, Renovation, Adaptive Reuse, February.

Oliveres i Guixer, M. 2018. "Ville-Port Saint-Nazaire (France), 2001. New Plan for the Port of Saint-Nazaire: Restructuring a Former Submarine Base for Public Use and Regeneration of Its External Spaces." *Public Space* (blog). February 5.

Pacciardi, G. 2019. "The History and Evolution of the Pigalle Duperré Court." Design. *Collateral* (blog). 2019. https://www.collater.al/en/the-history-and-evolution-of-the-pigalle-duperre-court/.

Perczel, A., and E. Lábass. 2007. *Unprotected Heritage: Residential Buildings in the Jewish Quarter*. Város Arcai. Városháza.

Picon, G. 2021. *The Bourse de Commerce: An Architectural Tour*. Pinault Collection. Editions Tallandier.

Pinault Foundation. 2021. "La Bourse de Commerce - The New Museum of the Pinault Collection. Architecture and Heritage." Press Release.

Pontecaille, P. 2020. "Chroniques / Le terrain Duperré à Pigalle (75009) : entre démarche citoyenne, outil commercial et levier de marketing urbain." *Urbanités* (March 30). https://www.revue-urbanites.fr/chronique-pontecaille-2020/.

Séron-Pierre, C. 2007. "ALVEOLE 14, Saint-Nazaire. Amenagement d'un Equipement Culturel Dans La Base Des Sous-Marins." *Le Moniteur*, January 6. https://www.lemoniteur.fr/article/alveole-14-saint-nazaire.430049.

Solá Morales, M. de. 2008. "Ville Port, Saint Nazaire The Historic Periphery." *Architectural Design* 78 (1): 88–93. https://doi.org/10.1002/ad.616.

THERE IS POTENTIAL IN *POTENTIAL*

Wording and knowledge construction in architecture

Matteo Robiglio

How many times do architects leave a site visit, a meeting, or a presentation where the word "potential" has been widely used, referring to the physical, geographical, economic, cultural etc. context in which architecture is expected to define the features of a transformation from the past to the future? The potential of a location, the potential of a layout, the potential of a material, the potential of a technology...

The word is not specific to architecture terminology. It is listed neither in the very established *Oxford Dictionary of Architecture* nor in the trendier *Architecture Dictionary*. Any browser will list about 3 billion online recurrences for "potential," while a relatively common architectural term like "plinth" occurs around 15 million times. I suspect that the use of the term potential has increased after the turn of the millennium, and that this increase is related to the growing role of reuse in architectural practice and debate: as reuse starts from a pre-existing situation, whose features (site, typology, structure, envelope, space, layout, matter, etc.) influence, if not determine, the characteristics of the projects that will transform this situation. I might prove wrong, but I cannot remember Le Corbusier, Gropius, or Loos using this term. Landscape architect Lancelot Brown (1716–1783) apparently used its synonym "capability" so often that it became his nickname—but this proves the exceptionality of his case.

Creating specialist terminology, distinct from common language, is one of the fundamental steps in defining a realm of knowledge and/or practice. Isn't it?
In the introduction to his 1959 book *Words of Science, and the History Behind Them*, popular science and sci-fi author Isaac Asimov complained that the permanence of common words like "work" in scientific disciplines such as physics made concepts confusing and difficult to learn—since many of the activities we would call "work" do not produce "work" in the sense of displacement force. Therefore, openness, indetermination, polysemy etc. are deficiencies that need to be remedied.

On the contrary, in 1986 Christian Girard devotes his entire book *Architecture et concepts nomades: traité d'indiscipline*—published at a time of prolific yet often equivocal exchanges, with architects trying to read René Thom on catastrophes or Maturana & Varela on autopoiesis—to advocating exactly the opposite, recognizing the specificity of architecture precisely in its indeterminate disciplinary boundaries and its openness to the incorporation of common terms and terms from other fields of knowledge/practice, often through a metaphorical—thus inherently non-disciplinary and non-disciplined—use.

Are we therefore condemned to choose between precision and fertility, between measure and imagination?

This book focuses instead on the possibility of bridging and connecting, thus positively framing the notion of potential for architectural designers both as a powerful conceptual metaphor with a rich historical, cross-cultural heritage that encompasses philosophy, poetry, art, and science, and as a powerful analytical tool that can help us with the task of structuring the design processes of adaptive reuse, making them comparable and, in some aspects, even measurable.

After exploring the semantic interdisciplinary scope of the term, Elena Guidetti leads us into the exploration of 16 case studies, selected as examples of the variety of reuse situations that well represent a post-functional operational state in which the situation "as is" can be analyzed for its remaining features rather than for its original programs or promises, lost in the wreckage of interrupted use and care. Retracing the many different possible paths from loss to reuse, a second bridge is built between past and future, encapsulated in the proposed definition of "transformative potential," meaning that the features of the remaining past already contain the ingredients of the future that can be activated through design interventions.

Those features are identified, described with drawings and schemes, and, where possible, measured, using the converging approaches of morphology, layering, and embodied energy. Three well-established disciplinary methodologies: the first stems from modern architectural theory and history, while the second and third are more recent by-products of cybernetics—with computer-assisted drawing—and ecology—with the extension of energy and life-cycle assessment to built legacies. These three methodologies are merged here to describe, compare, and evaluate the relationship between pre-existing situation and designed transformation produced by a set of recurring deconstruction and reconstruction actions, showing how the specificity of each situation and the individuality of each designer nevertheless lead to a taxonomy of recognizable classes/attitudes of intervention.

The path from general concept to individual designs thus leads to a (limited) generalization of approaches, tools, and devices. In this way, the book provides not only a hopefully useful contribution to the debate on conservation, preservation, reuse, and transformation of urban legacies, but also a potentially replicable example of how architecture can construct its own contemporary terminology, frame emerging issues, relate to neighboring research fields, and develop quantitative approaches to quality, without betraying its constitutive commitment to practice and the consequent care and healing of the uniqueness of each specific situation we inherit from the past and bring into the future.

In this new wording possibility lies a non-negligible part of the potential of this book.

THE POTENTIAL OF
FORM

HOW TO TRANSFORM
EXISTING BUILDINGS IN
POST-FUNCTIONAL EUROPE

Cover:
Images and graphics:
Design and setting:
Production:
Lithography:
Copy editing:
Project management:

© 2025 by jovis Verlag
An imprint of Walter de Gruyter GmbH, Berlin/Boston
Texts by kind permission of the authors.
Pictures by kind permission of the photographers/holders of the picture rights.
All rights reserved.

Can Sau, designed by Un Parell d'Arquitectes
Elena Guidetti
Floyd E. Schulze
Susanne Rösler
Bild1Druck
Bianca Murphy
Franziska Schüffler

Printed in the European Union.
For questions about the General Product Safety Regulation please contact
productsafety@degruyterbrill.com.

Bibliographic information published by the Deutsche Nationalbibliothek
The Deutsche Nationalbibliothek lists this publication in the Deutsche Nationalbibliografie;
detailed bibliographic data are available on the Internet at
http://dnb.d-nb.de

jovis Verlag
Genthiner Straße 13
10785 Berlin

www.jovis.de

jovis books are available worldwide in select bookstores. Please contact your nearest
bookseller or visit www.jovis.de for information concerning your local distribution.

ISBN 978-3-98612-170-9 (softcover)
ISBN 978-3-98612-171-6 (e-book)

This book was made possible by the kind support of the Future *Urban Legacy* Lab (F*UL*L)
and the Department of Architecture and Design (DAD) at Politecnico di Torino.

The ongoing project "Atlas of Potential" provides additional data:
https://www.atlasofpotential.com/